BE *a* MAN *of* **STANDING**

BE *a* MAN *of* STANDING

How to be
SUPERMAN
in a Clark Kent World

JIM MOORE

New York

BE *a* MAN *of* STANDING
How to be SUPERMAN *in a Clark Kent World*

Published in New York, New York, by Morgan James Publishing. Morgan James and The Entrepreneurial Publisher are trademarks of Morgan James, LLC.
www.MorganJamesPublishing.com

The Morgan James Speakers Group can bring authors to your live event. For more information or to book an event visit The Morgan James Speakers Group at
www.TheMorganJamesSpeakersGroup.com.

A **free** eBook edition is available
with the purchase of this print book.

CLEARLY PRINT YOUR NAME ABOVE IN UPPER CASE

Instructions to claim your free eBook edition:
1. Download the BitLit app for Android or iOS
2. Write your name in **UPPER CASE** on the line
3. Use the BitLit app to submit a photo
4. Download your eBook to any device

ISBN 978-1-63047-679-3 paperback
ISBN 978-1-63047-680-9 eBook
ISBN 978-1-63047-681-6 hardcover
Library of Congress Control Number:
2015909395

Cover Design by:
Rachel Lopez
www.r2cdesign.com

Interior Design by:
Bonnie Bushman
The Whole Caboodle Graphic Design

In an effort to support local communities and raise awareness and funds, Morgan James Publishing donates a percentage of all book sales for the life of each book to Habitat for Humanity Peninsula and Greater Williamsburg.

Get involved today, visit
www.MorganJamesBuilds.com

Habitat
for Humanity
Peninsula and
Greater Williamsburg
Building Partner

TABLE OF CONTENTS

Acknowledgements

To say that I am honored and yet humbled to be chosen to write this book and start this movement would be an extreme understatement. Yet God in His great mercy, grace and love has called me to do so therefore I really have no other choice. I first want to thank my Heavenly Father for showing me He has called each of us to come onto the scene as partners in His nature and be men of standing and that's what I'm in hot pursuit to becoming.

I want to thank Bruce Barbour, my literary agent, who grasped the Man of Standing message and has confirmed this is a message that must quickly go around the world. You have come along beside me, Bruce. You have led me, encouraged me, mentored me, and challenged me to be the man, especially during this publishing process.

To the incredible people at Morgan James Publishing who also caught the vision and have done an amazing job getting the message out.

To Ken Canfield, the founder of the National Center for Fathering, who pushed me through some dark days to teach me this is a message all men need to hear.

To Peter Spokes whose last words to me have been an instrument of perseverance. To some really great friends T-Bob, Ricky T, and Jim B who have always been there for me with prayers, encouraging words and a chicken dinner when needed.

To my dad, who from my earliest times of my memory of him till the day he took his last breath instilled in me the love and sacrifice for family. I love you dad!

To my children, Ryan, Lauren and Maddie. You have walked this mission with me all the way through, on good and bad days, and you were always there for me. You're incredible!

And to Liz, the absolute love of my life. You sometimes asked me while we were on this journey if Sara the wife of Abraham had any say about their life's path as God spoke to her husband while their unusual journey was taking place. Yet you believed in me…even through the darkest of dark hours. You have been so gracious. My goal is to be that Man for you. You deserve it.

To all the dedicated fathers who have served as a Watchdog over the years, making a difference in their kid's lives. Come on over to this new movement also and let's go change the world.

And last and most of all to my Papa, His Son and His Spirit. You have created a life that is greater than anything we can ask or even imagine! I believe it. I have tasted just a little portion of it and it is truly is a tree of life. Please use this book as a message that dramatically awakens men everywhere to the life that awaits them; a life that will bring your Kingdom into their marriages and their families.

INTRODUCTION

A few things I want to share with you before you begin this journey. I know there are some authors who can sit down and write a book in a few weeks or have their ghostwriter do it for them from their notes. I am neither. This awakening has been a long journey that first exploded in my soul in 2000 and has continued to gain traction and energy in my heart and soul almost daily.

As I am finishing the manuscript nearly 15 years later, I have had a lot of time to think about what to say and how to say it. I want this to be a spiritual encounter with the Father and His Son and His Spirit; a revolution among men that breaks out around the world, and not just "another book" that's a gift from someone or something you buy in a bookstore. I don't want it to end up like most other books that you've read or if you're like most men, read a few pages and then put it on a shelf and forget about it forever. I want this to be something that changes your thinking and actions in such a way that the life and destiny that has been written for you won't be missed but will instead be manifested. My passion is that as men we stop this endless wandering around in the desert, choking and starving for our manhood to reappear and that we'll finally awaken to the magnificent mission that we've all been given.

So there are a couple of final thoughts before your turn the page. First, I'm not the guru of guru's on this subject. So now you're asking, "Then why would you write this book and why have I spent money buying it?" Simple. Because God called me to and He has not stopped bugging me about it since He planted it in my heart years ago. I don't know why He called me to start Watch D.O.G.S. but He did and millions of men and kids have been positively impacted by an incredible program. I didn't seek it out. He sought me out and all I did was say, "Yes" and He's done the rest, including bringing on some wonderful team mates who helped craft and deliver the vision and mission. To all of you, I say, "Thank you and God bless you."

I wasn't an expert on education or father involvement. I was simply a father who wanted to be involved in my children's education. And the same is true with this "Spiritual Testosterone" movement. As much as I want to be Superman all the time, it doesn't mean that it's a reality for me all the time. Sometimes I stink at it and that's one of the reasons it's taken me so long to write this book. Without question, there have been many times I've wanted to throw it all in the trash and just be a guy who gets lost in the crowd because I don't always fly like Superman. Sometimes I was so Clark Kent and got easily discouraged. That was until God showed up one day and spoke these words to my spirit. He said, "Live the book your writing and not write the book you're living." In other words, "Write what I tell you to and then go live it." That liberated me. I trust it will liberate you.

Second, there are a lot of actions points in this book that you must begin to implement into your life and marriage. You'll discover that passivity and neglect have been two of the stronger pillars of men throughout history that must be torn down and rebuilt with such a powerful manhood passion. These actions can change the direction for you and can magnetically draw your wife closer to you than ever. That will take some serious effort, period. But understand that these manhood acts of rightness or righteousness are actions that can rebuild and restore lost passions and relationship with your wife. They can put you back in right standing with her. But do not mistake these actions as something that must be done to be in right standing with God. Let me be perfectly clear. If you are a true, born again child of God then you are in right standing with Him whether you believe it or not or whether you act like it or not. Not because of your actions but because of the finished work of His Sons actions and what He did for you on the cross. So don't confuse the two.

Let me say it another way. I am in right standing with the Father but if I want to have sculptured pectoral muscles so my wife likes to see me in a swimsuit, then I need to be doing a ton of pushups and other chest work. It doesn't make God love me more but it shows Liz that I want to look my best for her and there's not one thing wrong with that. Likewise, these manhood actions that this book will lead you into have nothing to do with making God love you more or anything else that performance base acceptance teaching has erroneously taught us in the past. God loves you perfectly as you are right now. Whether you're in the midst of an incredible marriage or in the middle of a seemingly inescapable ditch, God loves you perfectly and is rooting for you and cheering you on to live life to the fullest…if you're His child. And if you're not, then I invite you to enter into a love relationship with Him through His Son, Jesus Christ and let Him navigate you back to where you need to be.

So let's get started on this journey. Turn up your testosterone and turn the page.

CHAPTER 1

THE JOURNEY
BEGINS

I t was August, 2000. My wife Liz, our three kids, and I were on a beach in Panama City, Florida. We had not taken a family vacation in five years, but we managed to save just enough to have some beach time. I had recently left my profession of 14 years. I felt called by God to start a fathering initiative named Watch D.O.G.S. because school shootings were happening across our country all too often. The acronym for D.O.G.S. stands for Dads of Great Students and it's a program where fathers, grandfathers, uncles, or men of the home come to school for two reasons. To be an extra set of eyes and ears, and to be a positive male role model. Because of a couple different economic events we had seen our finances depleted. We had $137.06 in our corporate checking account to run this "world changing movement," and not much more in our personal account either. I chose to jump in, obey God, and follow Him on this path. Although we were not new in our overall faith, we were rookies for a life and walk based on faith and not on sight.

We had lived the typical American life going for the typical American dream, and at this particular time in our lives things were not going quite like we wanted. With the stress of starting a new venture and not enough money to make it, enjoying the life that was in front of us was difficult. We loved one other, but when a man gets a vision from God to go off and start a crazy idea to change the world, his wife and kids are dragged along that road too. Any marriage and home would be challenged, and ours was no different.

I couldn't help but think, *it's not supposed to be this way God. I didn't sign up for this. When I said yes to your call to revolutionize men's lives and turn them to their families, it was supposed to be nothing but a bed of roses!* Surely my wife and kids would see the valor in something like this, and even though stress was breaking things in two, they would still be at peace 100% of the time...*right God*?

Stress of any kind is disruptive. Financial stress can be devastating because it affects everything you do. When the tank gets empty or the lake dries up you get a chance to see all the junk at the bottom, and that described me. I had absolutely no self-esteem. I felt like a failure. My circumstances and the enemy of my soul screamed out at me that I was a failure. To make matters worse, I acted like I was a failure. I didn't really have a lot to say to Liz because I knew this wasn't what she signed up for either. It was about this time I found myself crying out on the beach for another word from God. This time though, I needed one that was going to be an answer to our dilemma—a word that would be everything I needed to get me and my family back to where we were supposed to be.

Sometimes God has a really weird sense of humor. You're calling out to the Almighty for an answer and you think you're going to get some magnificent Hollywood special-effects-like response, and all you get are three little words...Boaz and Ruth.

I had enough Bible in me to know the basics of the story. Some guy name Boaz did something and redeemed some woman name Ruth and he was a good guy. Okay God, how does this pay my bills? How does this earn back my wife's respect? How does this make me into the conquering champion I so desire to be? Surely all of these wishes can't be wrapped up into three little words?

I began to read the story and I was fascinated with how the NIV translation labeled Boaz. It tagged him as a "Man of Standing." The King James Version calls him a "Mighty Man of Wealth." Both sounded cool, but I was really intrigued with the sound of Man of Standing. I read of the encounter of Ruth and Boaz. How a broken down woman who had lost everything found life, hope, and the man of her dreams. That's what I wanted. I wanted to be that kind of man. When I found out what the word "standing" meant in the Hebrew language—a force of Men, means, resources, wealth, virtue, valor, strength and ability—I wanted it even more! That day, things changed in my life forever. That day I discovered God had painted a picture for all men to strive for. That day He revealed to me that He is extremely passionate about each of us walking and living out this "manhood DNA" He has placed in us. That day, I set out on a new road—the road that would take my family back to the way it was supposed to be.

Things began to change and the organization He called me to start began to explode. In a few years it became the largest safe school, fathering initiative in the country. The promises He had given me at the very beginning, were unfolding before us on a daily basis. Life was sweet again. The people we were meeting and the places we were going were off the charts. Then one day He called me to leave the office and drive to a particular place because there was something He wanted to share with me. He took me to the Book of Ruth, and that hour He opened up my heart and let me see things in this story about Boaz and Ruth I had never seen before. Things I didn't even realize were possible. It seemed like I was there in my vehicle for a thousand years, and when it was over I knew I could never be the same again.

> *Every man wants to be pursued by his wife but every woman wants her husband to be pursuit worthy.*

What Boaz had, I wanted. What he did, I wanted to do. It hit me so hard that this beautiful woman who had been destroyed by the circumstance of life, in the matter of one chapter, had a complete reversal of her situation. She was passionately pursuing the man of her dreams. I thought, what if we as men could live out this life Boaz possessed? What if we became the true champions we were created to be? What if we could tap into God's strength and awaken men around the world with the truth that God designed us with the same potential Boaz used to become a champion? Every man wants to be pursued by his wife but every woman wants her husband to be pursuit worthy. It became amazingly clear. That's what I wanted too. That's what I wanted to be. I became obsessed. Not passionate, because passion is an overused, under lived word. I became radical. I wanted to live it in my own life and lead others to the same burning desire. No more of the status quo, I wanted it the way it's supposed to be. I wanted to be a Man of Standing. That day, my life and its direction changed forever. My passion for Watch D.O.G.S. paled in comparison to what I felt for this Man of

Standing stuff. I ate, drank, slept, breathed, and sometime bled for this mission of men in schools; but, I knew, from that time forward, there was a new call, a new dream, and a new direction.

It's one thing to receive a vision and a corresponding promise, but it's so much sweeter when those seemingly impossible promises manifest themselves. Life was good. Life was smooth. That's where we were…until one Sunday morning.

I got up early that day to spend some quiet time alone, just listening to God. I found myself in the book of Genesis and the story of Noah. Like most, I have read this story countless times, seen it depicted on television, heard about it from the time I was born. This time there was something inside me that wouldn't let go. I read how God instructed Noah to take his wife, their three kids and their kid's spouses, and build this 882-foot vessel. I found out that even though the rains came for forty days, they stayed on the Ark together for one year. I realized that when Noah walked out of the Ark, the world was his for the taking. He was in charge. He could set precedents and lead. In short, he was *The Man*. Sitting there in the front room of our house I knew these words were for me. God had shown up there with me.

I began to journal everything He was placing in my heart. Before He was finished speaking, I knew He was calling me to leave the organization I had founded. He told me He wanted me to build an ark for my family. Not a literal ark in my front yard, but He was calling me to build something just for my family and to be in it and nothing else for one year. I had spent all this time traveling, telling fathers how to be good and to always be there for their families, and now He was telling me that this new road was for me. Build the ark, take your family inside, and shut the doors behind you; and for one year let this be everything! In other words, for the next year I was supposed to pour everything I had into my own home. Build the Ark!

A few days later He led me to the book, Haggai in the Old Testament. It seemed as if many times there was major transition about to occur in my life He has taken me to this book. The premise in this story is simple. God's people weren't serious about their relationship with Him. They were focused on their own lives with their own agendas, and God was well down on their list of priorities. Once again, The Almighty showed up and told them to "Go up into the mountains, bring down timber, and build the house." Build Me a house I can get involved in and take glory in! God was telling them to build Him something He could bless. Those words went down so deep into my spirit and soul that again, I knew they were for me. So, here I am…between building an ark, and going up into the mountains, bringing down timber and building a house. It was extremely clear that I was supposed to be building something. Everyday—literally everyday—God was in my face telling me to "Go up into the mountains, bring down timber and build the house…Go up into the mountains, bring down timber and build the house." It was wearing me out.

During spring break of that year we took the kids snow skiing in the mountains of Colorado. Liz and I were both sold to the fact that God was calling me to leave; but neither of us knew what it really looked like, and the purpose still wasn't clear. All I knew was I was supposed to "go up into the mountain, bring down timber," and build something. During the trip we contracted folliculitis from the hot tub in the house. For me it came up as little pimples, but for our son who had been ill with a stomach disorder for some time, it looked like infected golf balls coming out of his underarms. Liz found a doctor's clinic near the ski resort and took the kids to it, leaving me to spend some much needed time in prayer. Life was now stress on steroids! My child had endured a lengthy illness, my mother had been diagnosed with cancer, and now I felt called to leave an organization we had poured our lives into. Watch D.O.G.S. was having so much success and the blessings were abounding. Now I was supposed to build something, but I had no clue how to start, much less what to construct.

I sat on the bed on the third story of this beautiful house with my back against the headboard asking God questions. *How are we going to survive? How are we going to pay for this? Why are you asking me to go down this road again?*

For those of you who don't believe in the supernatural here is where you're going to get a little uncomfortable. As I am trying to teach God that money doesn't grow on trees, and that we can't possibly survive while I'm in this ark and building this house, I hear a large truck coming down the mountain. Let me make this extremely clear. We are in the mountains, in a house, far from any business. I'm curious what type of truck is making its way down snow covered roads. It's an armored truck! You know the kind that carries tons of money in it and delivers it to banks. I watch this thing slowly come down the mountain and pull right into the driveway of the house where we're staying! I kid you not. Not a single person got out or in the truck. It just sat in the driveway motionless. It stayed there for a few moments longer, then slowly backed out of the driveway. It slowly drove away from the house allowing me to clearly see what it was. I walked back to my bed and I started to laugh as God began to tell me in my heart that I'm not supposed to worry about money. I'm simply supposed to follow Him down this new road, and if He has to bring a money truck to the mountains of Colorado to pay our bills, He'll do just that.

I sat back down on the bed with my back against the headboard knowing that was the number one most incredible "God showing up in front of my face" experience I could remember…until ten seconds later when number two showed up.

I looked up and at the foot of my bed. There sat an angel. Okay, now let's get this straight. I grew up in a denomination that thought angels were babies in loin clothes, and were painted on the pages of old bibles. I knew they were real but never believed in this lifetime I would ever see one. But that day, in that room, on that bed, it happened. Please don't be offended by this, but if you don't believe me about this I couldn't care less. It happened.

This angel looked right into my eyes and simply smiled with a countenance of peace I had never experienced. Without saying a word he let me know everything we were going through was going to be okay. He looked up just over the top of my head as if he were focused on whatever it was that was there and began to move his eyes from my eyes to whatever was behind me. Back and forth. Several times. It was clear there was something just behind me and just over my head he wanted me to see…and then he was gone. I turned around and on the wall directly behind me was a mural hanging over the bed. On it was a picture of a beautiful home in the mountains that had been built by the timber from the mountain. The words immediately came to my spirit, "Go up into the mountains, bring down timber and build the house." The angel had not said a single word, nor did he tell me what I was supposed to build. That came at a later date. But it became perfectly clear that day that God was extremely serious about me leaving the path I was on and to join Him in a new work, in a new direction, and He would take care of us every step of the way.

I told the Lord that if He was serious and this really was His will, I wasn't going to start until I could save one year's worth of expenses. We sowed a seed, believed Him for it, and He provided for two years. I was hoping my demands would have slowed down His request some, but it was evident to both of us He was ready for me to start now. In August of that year that's exactly what I did. I left what I once thought would be the ultimate vocational passion of my life. I had no roadmap other than His call to listen to Him, build an ark—build a house—and get on the road that would lead me to His life of Standing.

We were about to embark on a journey that would prepare us for this book. We had no clue about where we were going. I really felt a little like Abraham in Genesis 11, and God was telling me to leave everything and go to a new land, and when you get there I'll tell you what I want you to do. Not a lot of comfort if you ask me, but it was a trip we had to take. A journey that turned into a four-year trip. The first two years were pretty easy, but not a lot of things seemed to facilitate the direction of this new movement. God was speaking but it was more about reconnecting with my family as He had asked me to do. The last two years were just the opposite. The harvest was gone. Our savings were gone! The only thing that was different was that God was speaking louder than ever before and His message was simple. "Listen to Me daily. Do not pay any attention to your circumstances. Trust me explicitly, and even if your savings goes to zero, do not under any circumstances quit and give up on this journey. You are to seek out this Boaz life and live it at all times. The teaching would come later. First must come the journey to discover it and taste it.

Ruth 1:7 is where Ruth and her mother-in-law Naomi make a decision. When you read the account of Ruth you'll immediately discover that Ruth had lost her husband. Her mother-in-law was determined to travel back to the land of Judah that she and her late husband had left some time earlier when a drought hit the area. Ruth had a decision to make. Stay in Egypt or go somewhere new. She chose to embark on a new journey with Naomi. Verse 7 is incredible. It says, "She left the place where she had been living and set out on the road that would take her back to Judah." Judah represented the land where she and Naomi were supposed to be. It was a land for the children of God to occupy and dominate. It was a land where she would find her dream and her dream man, but first there was a road she must travel. It was a road she had never been on before; a road that would take them back to the land of Judah.

We don't know anything about this road. Was it long or short? Was it easy or treacherous? Who would they meet along the way? It was probably some of each, but here's what we know: They both got on the road and didn't stop until they made it to Judah. That is what *Man of Standing* is all about. This book serves as a roadmap that is written solely to get you and me to this land of Standing.

This is about the road that God led me on for you. There were times when the wind blew hard and life didn't make any sense. There were times where I had intimate moments with God like I'd never experienced before. There were times when God was speaking and His will and His word were crystal clear, and there were times when it was so difficult that I wasn't sure I could take my next breath. There were times I wanted to quit. There were times I lashed out at

God. But every time I walked to the edge of what I thought might be the breaking point, He showed up with His mercy, grace, and His comfort to give me the right word and the right miracle to make it another day.

At one point God took me to the book of Exodus, where the children of Israel had been set free from Egypt and they were headed for the Promised Land. The only problem was God told Moses He was going to take them on a longer route so they would not engage in a battle with an enemy and quit. He kept them right on the edge of the desert as they followed the road. Ultimately He set them by mountains on one side and a sea on another—the absolute worst place to be if you were faced with a battle. Yet, God had a plan and it was for their good and His glory. That's where I felt I was every day for a couple years, traveling the long way at the edge of a barren desert, every step of the way. There were mountains on one side and a sea on the other. Friends and even family were looking at us thinking, *Jim has lost his mind. They have no money and everyday he gets in his truck, drives to a remote location and listens to God.* During those two years the Lord asked me to do some really off-the-wall, non-traditional kinds of things, like faith walks around a lake proclaiming scripture when everyone else was working, all night prayer-a-thons, or a 21-day fast, and those were just a few of the easy ones. But this was my journey. This was my road. He had to place me in an absolutely desperate and totally dependent place where I would have nothing or anyone to trust in besides Him. There were days it was dry, barren, and dangerous. There were days where Liz and I looked at each other and both wondered if I truly had lost my mind. And yet there were days where He showed up like that angel on my bed and placed His words into my life that were so alive and so powerful it literally took

It's time to have every dream and desire of our hearts fully satisfied. It's time to see it all come into reality. It's time to get back on the road. The road that leads us back to the way God designed it to be.

my breath away. There were also days He gave me visions—pulled back the curtain on my life—and let me see the way it's supposed to be. And it's the obsession of turning those visions into reality that drives what I do each day.

There was a road Naomi and Ruth had to travel to get them to the place they were supposed to be. There was a road I had to travel to show me how it can be and there will be a road for you to travel as well. Some will be longer and more difficult than others. That will be determined by where you start your journey. There will be days that are incredible and filled with joy, and there might be some days that will bring more than you think you can handle, filled with doubts and discouragement.

The choice to travel down this road is totally up to you. You have to ask yourself this question: "Am I going to stay where I am in my present circumstances, or am I willing to get back on the road that

That's your choice, and whatever you decide will determine your destiny.

will take me back to the promise land?" That's your choice, and whatever you decide will determine your destiny.

There really is a road that can lead us as men to a life we've only dreamed about—a life where we are passionately pursued by our wives because we have become pursuit worthy; a life of being a God anointed champion; a life of living the way it's supposed to be—as a force of men, means, resources, and wealth; filled with virtue, valor, and strength.

Stop worrying about what other people might think about God's will for your life. If they don't agree, it's their problem not yours. God may call you to do something completely outside of all of your training and your comfort zone in order to rebuild your marriage and your family. You've got to determine that you're going to work at it with all your heart. It will take extra work, extra detail, extra prayer, extra encouragement, and extra power. But if you persevere long enough, you too can taste of the destiny waiting and created for you.

You're going down this road which can be difficult and treacherous at times, but you're traveling on it for your marriage and your family. As Men of Standing we must be steadfast, no matter how long it takes, how crazy it sounds, how hard it seems, or how much you feel you're the only one on it. You must commit to rising up and seeing yourself becoming all you were created to be. It's all about the road. Are you ready for the trip?

It's time to reclaim what is ours. It's time to have the marriage and family we have only dreamed about. It's time to have every dream and desire of our hearts fully satisfied. It's time to see it all come into reality. It's time to get back on the road. The road that leads us back to the way God designed it to be.

CHAPTER 2

THE WAY IT'S
SUPPOSED TO BE

T his book is about manhood. It drips with testosterone. This book is written for every man, especially for those who are sick and tired of the typical predictable, mundane, routine, broken down, weak, boring rut we call being the typical man. We secretly ask the question to ourselves but never openly to anyone else, *Is this it?*

What you're about to read is for men who have an obsession to live an authentic life and to taste all the sweet fruits of success and conquest. This blows past passion and screams straight to obsession. You eat, sleep, drink, breathe, get out of bed, and long for it to be real. It's the obsession to be a real man. A Superman.

God placed this into the heart and soul of every man. It is a must that is mapped in our DNA. It is burned and branded into our very core, but is a fire that no longer burns as hot as it should. It's found in every cell of our body, yet we fail to breathe it and exist in it fully. Being a real man—THE man—defines everything about us and controls the way we think. It directs everything we do and dictates how we react. When we are not in it full throttle, at maximum capacity, our lives tilt off their axes and we stutter, sputter, and limp.

Many men fail to step into this God created design. Society consistently tries to reverse it. Churches tragically attempt to dilute it. Some even try to surgically remove it but none truly can because it's perfectly crafted into every strand of a man's DNA and it can never leave us, even though most will never fully embrace it. If you find you're in this place now, follow the roadmap laid out in these pages and get out of it before your destiny of a true, authentic champion is lost and possibly never to be experienced.

When I read the accounts of men throughout the ages who through faith conquered kingdoms and gained what was promised; who shut the mouths of lions and quenched the fury of the flames; whose weakness was turned to strength, and who became powerful in battle; who created wealth and abundance; who changed cultures; who were heroes to their families, greatly desired by their wives, and were leaders among men; I am blown away by the size of the gulf of what I have lived versus what has been within my reach. Get this now. God designed men to be conquerors. Virtuous leaders who not only command but earn respect. Our kids long to be like them, and our wives long to be with them. These are the ones God calls Men of Standing.

What you are reading will open your eyes to what God says about the way manhood should really be. When you're finished, it will be etched on your soul that you are to be a force! A provider. A protector. A romantic magnet. A champion of strength and of valor. A real man who definitely looks the part and divinely lives the part—spiritually, physically, financially, and romantically. The total package! Not only will you discover that this life is possible, but that it is the way it's supposed to be. This is not story-book fluff. This is serious stuff for serious men. For you who are single it can help you win the love of your future wife; and for those who are married, it can help you win back and strengthen her love. This is for real, but it's up to you to follow this map for your intended destiny.

When I was a kid I had several heroes, but none could top my desire to be Superman—not just to be like him—I wanted to be him! I dressed like him and tried to walk and talk like him. My parents bought me a Superman costume and I even tried to fly like him. That one cost me a trip to the emergency room to sew my tongue back together. I'll never forget that my costume had a disclaimer on it that read, "Remember: This costume won't make you fly, only Superman can fly." I wish I had believed that before I jumped from the coffee table to the sofa! But never did I realize how powerful those few small words were then and how powerful they are now. A costume won't make you fly. Only Superman can fly! In the beginning of the film *Superman,* he travels to Earth as an infant while his father tells him of his destiny among men. He grows up and works to change everything around him for the better, and he wins the heart of the woman of his dreams. The same holds true today. The costume of being a typical, boring, run of the mill man that hides our true identity won't and can't make us fly. It's only when we are living out our own destiny that was spoken into us by our Heavenly father on our way to this planet, that we will be able to change the world for good and win the hearts of our wives. Just remember, mild mannered Clark Kent never won the heart of Lois Lane. Why couldn't she see that Clark was really Superman? A pair of stupid looking glasses and a different part in his hair were all that separated Clark from Superman. Surely Lois, could see it was him. (I know it's Hollywood here, but work with me.) The truth is, it was more than just glasses and a different hairdo. It was the inner man, the ultimate champion hiding on the inside of Clark Kent waiting to be unleashed. But all she could see was mild mannered Clark Kent. He was clumsy, goofy, and weak. But when the need arose and the shirt was ripped off, this Man of Steel—this Man of Standing—was unleashed, evil was demolished, and romance was established. His enemies ran from him and the love of his life ran to him. That's what we all want. That's what we all scream for on the inside, and if you're not screaming for it right now then you're worse off. You've become more like Jimmy Olsen, the news reporter who longed to be like Superman but thought that kind of adventure and romance was for someone else and not someone like him. The life of Superman! That's the way it's supposed to be! That's what we can all have. Remember this, the Superman suit and his true identity was always there, it was just covered by the clumsy clothes and goofy glasses. The same holds true with us today. Our true identity of as The Man of Standing is always with us. It's just been covered up and disguised by our own set of weak, clumsy clothes. Who do you want to be and what do you want to have? To be mild-mannered Clark Kent or experience the adventures of Superman? The choice is yours. I'm calling you out Superman. Take off your weak, clumsy costume. Wake up!

Here's the advantage Superman had. He had a father who took the time to speak to his son and tell him who he truly was.

He communicated what his true name meant and what he was destined to do. Superman's Kryptonian name was "Kal-el" which closely resembles the Hebrew word for "voice of God." The "el" at the end of his name means "of God." It is also found in other names of superhuman real life beings such as Gabriel and Ariel. Kal-el, or Superman, always knew in his gut that he was unique and blessed. Therefore, his first step into manhood was to listen to his father as he passionately spoke into him his identity and his mission, and so it is with us.

The words of a father. They either bring life or death. The words of Superman's father brought life. Chances are yours didn't. If so, great! For the majority of men this wasn't the case. So let me serve as your father and let me speak over you and into you the words you not only need to hear, but also long to hear. Better yet, let me speak over you the words of the Ultimate Father—the Father to even the fatherless, and let them resonate within you and show you what He actually says about you.

You're created in His image and you are to lead, to rule, and to win. Not just win, you are to dominate—the playing your arch rivals on their own home field and beating them 1,000 to 0 kind of domination! You're a champion. You're a winner! You've been chosen by the Majestic Creator to win in this life. You're more than a conqueror! Not only have you been blessed, but you've been given every spiritual blessing imaginable. You're blessed going in and blessed going out. You're blessed in the city and blessed in the country. You will

> *You're created in His image and you are to lead, to rule, and to win. Not just win, you are to dominate—the playing your arch rivals on their own home field and beating them 1,000 to 0 kind of domination!*

see through the example of Boaz what a Man of Standing looks like, and the rich rewards that are bestowed on a man who vigorously pursues what God made him to be. You are created to win—not just to show up and play, but to win…if you know the author of all victory. And you were created to find Him and to know Him too.

With absolutely no apologies to self-deprecating people who want to preach that we're tragically and fatally flawed, God begs to differ. We're to be the head not the tail. We're to build fine houses, not just survive in small tents. We are to be possessors of unsearchable riches, tasting the sweet fruits of victory by living out a magnetic life as a man beyond anything we have ever dreamed of, much less experienced. And yes, our marriages are supposed to rock.

We have got to get a fresh vision and a new perspective on this manhood thing quickly. I was flying one night on a private jet and had the privilege to ride in the cockpit. Both the pilot and I had our headsets on and were talking about the incredible view from 32,000 feet at night. He suddenly pointed out my window toward a huge array of lights on the ground and said, "Look, there's Memphis," and then he pointed straight out the front windshield and said, "There's Little Rock." To the right, Memphis. Straight ahead, Little Rock. I could see them both at the same time. I was totally awed by being able to see two great cities that are almost 140 miles apart in one glance. I had driven that road at night countless times. Each trip was long and difficult. But that night, it was different. I had a much greater perspective. It didn't seem nearly as long or difficult. How could it? It was from a higher vantage point. That's exactly what we've got to do right now with this picture of manhood. We've got to see ourselves from a different, loftier angle. We have to begin to see ourselves as men the way God sees us. It's critical that we rise above all the ground clutter blocking our true image of ourselves as men and begin to see things as God sees them.

In the Job 42, after everything had happened, Job proclaimed he had come full circle and learned this lesson. He said, "My ears have heard of you but now my eyes have seen you." Tragically, the first half of that verse describes the majority of men today. We have heard all the sermons, yet still choose to live in mediocrity. It's time for a new vision. It's time for a new dream.

All of creation—our wives, our children, this world—groans for men of honor and virtue to reveal themselves because that's the intended order of the world. That's the way it's supposed to be. Get this. We were created to reign and rule, and creation is laboring, it's yearning for Men of Standing to arise and shine and to take the lead. And when we do, it brings things into alignment.

I have some family members who obviously have way too much time on their hands, they are really into genealogy and recreating our family tree. For some reason our genetic DNA is important to them. For me, I'm usually not into driving while looking in the rear view mirror. I find very little benefit in spending a lot of time rebuilding the past. From what I know about my ancestors, I'm not sure I want to know much more about them. Besides, I have a hard enough time getting along with the ones who are alive now! Nevertheless, I think there are a few occasions where looking at where we came from can be helpful.

Let's go all the way back in our tree to the very beginning, to the Garden. There, the majestic blueprint was crafted and communicated by the Ultimate Creator of all things. His plan was to create a man who would listen to his father. A man who would embrace the DNA of dominion that was dropped into his very core and would live it out to the fullest. Not only would he live it out, he would pass down to the next generation the knowledge of who their ancestors were and all they possessed.

We find this DNA being given to man in Genesis chapter 1. In verse 26 it says we were created in His image to rule over all the earth. The word rule means to have dominion or to dominate. In verse 28 He blessed them and said "Be fruitful, multiply, fill the earth and subdue it." There it is. God's first command to man. Now, here's a new twist that most have never considered. The majority of those who read this have been programmed and taught that He was simply telling Adam and Eve to go have a bunch of kids—to populate the earth. But a closer look at the Hebrew language brings out a much deeper and richer meaning.

The word "multiply" means "to be or become great…to be or become many…to be or become much…to be or become numerous." Not only was God talking quantity, He was talking quality also. He was telling them that He had blessed mankind with the ability to prosper in all things, and that we are to bear fruit in this life and to be great. Become many and populate the earth? Absolutely, but as we grow in number we are also to be great while doing so! With this greatness, we are to have dominion and rule the earth. That's our call, and nothing, absolutely nothing has changed God's mind on this matter. Rise up Man of Standing! We are called to have dominion and win the love and respect of our wives and family every day. Anything less than living out our God-given DNA is like trying to walk on ice. It's a journey filled with slipping and sliding as we try and gain our balance, and we ultimately end up flat on our backs.

As Men of Standing we must embrace our destiny. We must firmly grasp our genetic gifts and live them out fully. We are to be the champions of our homes and champions to our wives. This "dominion seed" of being great is planted in all of us. It's the seed that's a gift from God. This gift not only gives us the ability to possess the dreams and desires for our lives, it gives us the permission and the power to live them out everyday.

Face it, there's a burning in your gut that causes unrest and uneasiness to gnaw at you, and it won't be quenched by anything less than this majestic destiny being lived out. When we tap into the power of what God breathed into us we allow the magnetic poles in our lives to align themselves where we will live out the destiny established from the very beginning. Stop creating theologies that justify loss and wake up and realize God wants us to win with dominion.

Stop creating theologies that justify loss and wake up and realize God wants us to win with dominion.

Do you want further proof about how God feels about this? Two thousand years ago He sent His Son with a message of abundant life. Jesus Christ said He came that "we might have life and have to the full." That was His mission and message. He was saying He was going to make it possible for us to live a life far greater than anything we could ever comprehend. This ultimate Man of Standing said His plan for us was abundance. The word "abundance" in Greek is *perissos* and more than just abundance, it means "exceeding some number or measure or rank or need; over and above; more than is necessary; superadded; supremely; something further; more; much more than all." Now, attach the word manhood after that and dream of how it can be. Imagine adding *perissos* to your marriage, your romance, your home, your finances, and your body! How would that be? It's possible. Not only possible, it's the way it's supposed to be...if you're ready to take Him at His word. Sounds too go to be true, doesn't it? Let me prove to you that it's not.

My dad grew up dirt poor on a farm in the Panhandle of West Texas. They had no air conditioning, heat, or electricity. No carpet, wallpaper, or indoor plumbing. Most kids today would say, "What, no smart phones, laptops, or Facebook?" Imagine if a salesman walked up to my fathers farmhouse in the 1930's and tried to sell him on this notion: "One day soon, son, you're going to be able to have a device the size of your hand, and on this machine you can send electronic messages, take pictures, check your bank account, surf the internet, and, oh, by the way…make calls." What do you think he would have said? He, like everyone else 80 years ago would have said, "Well that could never happen because *it's too good to be true!*"

What would have happened if 150 years ago someone would have told people living at that time that a silver metal bird-like object weighing thousands of pounds would fly over 500 miles an hour over the ocean and take people to a different country within a matter of hours? You're right! You would have said it will never happen because, *it's too good to be true!* How about space travel? What about things such as speech recognition, satellite radio, LED TV's, semiconductor chips the size of a grain of rice, fast lines at the Department of Motor Vehicles (well, that one might really be too good to be true!)…the list goes on and on. Things we take for granted everyday are now grafted and accepted into our everyday lives and we think nothing of them. The truth of the matter is simple. Just because you've never experienced it doesn't mean that it's too good to be true! Just because you've never tasted it doesn't mean it doesn't exist! And just because you know of no one who's ever lived it doesn't mean you can't. What about eternal life in Heaven? Too good to be true? You had better hope not! I'll say it again. Jesus said He came to bring us a life that is super-abundant, more than we can ask or imagine, incalculable and incomprehensible, not just for a select few but available to all who choose to receive it and take Him at His word.

Your wife deserves the best spiritual, physical, financial, emotional, and romantic Man of Standing you can possibly be. A champion of virtue who will rise to the occasion and do whatever it takes to be that man for her. Go back to the honeymoon. Go back to those first few years of your marriage. Relive the oneness and the passion. It's possible to be there again if you want it badly enough and are willing to do something about it. God says in Psalms 103:5 that He will "satisfy your desires with good things so that your youth is renewed like the eagles."

> *Your wife deserves the best spiritual, physical, financial, emotional, and romantic Man of Standing you can possibly be.*

Today, stop functioning in the dysfunctional. As men we've messed up this manhood thing for too long. We've completely lost our direction. We have truly thought that this role-reversing, upside-down life we've been accustomed to is the norm. Stop it! From this day forward your whole life can change if you're willing to get out of the rut and follow this map.

Today, start fresh to know who you are and who you were created to be. Fully grasp that you are on a new mission to dominate and win. Begin to really live with an unquenchable obsession to pamper, pursue, provide, and protect your wife and your family. Realize that your wife would rather melt in your arms with ecstasy than collapse on the couch with exhaustion. Stop being deterred by what you presently see and become passionate about turning your dreams into reality.

Today, awaken yourself to the covenant power of wealth. Pursue it for the betterment of the world and the pampering of your wife. Become a leader and quit being a follower. Understand that as Men of Standing we don't have to rely on accountability partners to help us keep our promises. We possess at our very core the non-negotiable heart and soul of valor. Have the undying obsession to live out this limitless life for you, your wife, and your kids. Know that you ultimately live for an audience of one; but you lead, influence, and dramatically impact everyone you touch. Know to whom you've been given, and make it the beat of your heart to support her becoming everything she can be as well.

Today, stop trying to just be a nice guy. Become obsessed to be the total package. Know who you are. Know whose you are. Know the covenant promises you can have. Know your manhood DNA; but most of all, find and get to know the originator of it. He's been waiting on you to come to Him all along.

Today, start playing to dominate in life. As Men of Standing we live for the game. We do not need some outside motivation to get us going. We're not waiting for the *Rocky* theme song to start playing. We live for the victory. Although occasional inspirational speeches are great for the short term, Men of Standing already see the goal and pursue it with an unquenchable fire that makes all other men pale in comparison. We live by the motto, "Whatever it takes!"

It's now time to take off this clumsy costume we've all been hiding behind. It's time we fully embrace the life of Superman. It's time we show the world who we are and who we were created to be. It's time to wear the suit with honor and win back her love. It's time to live in the way it's supposed to be. Rise up Superman. Take off your apron, it's supposed to be a cape!

CHAPTER 3

THE PROBLEM
WITH MOST GUYS

I t's one of my favorite commercials of all time. It will go into the
television commercial hall of fame. The setting: a football game.
There's just been a close call that went against one of the teams,
and the coach on the wrong side of the call is going ballistic to the
power of twelve directly into the referee's ear. The ref is standing there
motionless with a blank stare, looking straight ahead with absolutely
no emotion and seemingly no life. It's as if he hears nothing at all.
The television announcers are having a field day at his expense with
comments like, "He's (the coach) beating him like a rented mule and
the ref is just tuning him out." They laugh as they ask, "Boy, where
do you train to take a beating like that?" Immediately the scene
switches to the same ref, this time sitting on his couch at home, in
street clothes not moving a muscle with the same blank stare, gazing

a million miles away. But this time the nuclear blast going off in his ear is coming from his wife with all the tenderness of a runaway jackhammer on steroids! She wants to know when the porch is getting painted and when the mailbox is getting fixed. The commercial ends with his out of control, maniacal wife screaming directly into his ear at the top of her voice demanding, "And would it hurt for you to say you love me once in a while!"

I just watched it again online and it's hilarious. This is the kind of commercial you watch five times and you laugh harder each time you see it. Then a few seconds later reality sets in as you begin to realize this is a perfect picture with what's wrong with the majority of marriages in the world today. Probably not to that degree of anger, but the underlying problem is there, and that quickly sobers up the laughter. And no ladies, this is not about you. Your work comes in chapter 10. This is about us.

A couple of quick thoughts about the commercial and its level of reality and I'm not talking about what takes place on the football field. That's a given. I'm talking about what's happening on the couch or better yet what has not happened on the couch that caused this wife to be so out of control.

Most, if not all of you guys are going to punt your responsibility down the field and say, "Wow, that guy married a real fill-in-the-blank!" and take absolutely no responsibility for her actions or better yet, her *reactions*! Go ahead and try that and see where that gets you. That attitude will buy you a one way ticket to that couch! As men here is what we must understand. This guy is sitting there motionless and it's not from the screaming! This guy is sitting there motionless because motionlessness and keeping his mouth closed are in his DNA and in his bloodline! They're in yours and mine too.

Now, before you slam the book shut because truth is a stubborn thing and you're having trouble accepting it consider this. Ask yourself two questions and give an honest answer. First of all, in your home who is loudest when the kids haven't finished their homework, the bills are too high, or the house is a mess…you are your spouse? Second, think of every married couple you know. Ask yourself the same question about their situation. You'll find the vast majority in the same shape. Now I know, there's going to be a few of you who read this part and sanctimoniously rebuke the enemy and disagree, are grateful to God that your wife has NEVER, EVER been anything to you other than perfect, sweet, and peaceful. If that's the case then God bless you. If you've been married for more than twelve hours go write a book and tell the rest of us how you worked out!

Because of our Clark Kent-like behavior the vast majority of women are put into the position of being the aggressor when it comes to responsibility, while we the males, the ones who are supposed to be the conquering champions are usually standing around with our thumb up our…well usually standing around. It's not because our wives want that role. You might think they do but deep down, and sometimes very deep down, in their heart is a person longing to be set free from a lifetime of pain. Remember, hurt people hurt people. It's the way it is, but it's not the way it's supposed to be.

But how did we get here? I know I've blamed just about everything from my own personal frustrations to world hunger on my wife. And if I can't blame everything on her then that pretty much leaves only one other person…her mother!

The truth is…it's me. In your home, it's pretty much you. But again, how did we get here? How has there become such a role reversal between the husband and wife to where everyday our world becomes more and more dysfunctional? It's easy. We are simply following the directions that are laid out for us not only by this generation but from generations before us. If we really want to get to the bottom of this whole gigantic mess, we can trace it back to the beginning. I mean the very beginning, as in the Garden of Eden.

Adam had it really good. Walking around, unashamed in all the untouched beauty God had given him. Perfection everywhere. Not a stitch of clothes in sight. It was like the world was a giant men's locker room! Adam is THE Man. God's creation. In charge of it all. He's the boss! He gets to name everything because he's the CEO of the world. Not bad for a guy with no formal education or experience! Plus, he gets to daily walk and talk about anything and everything with God.

One day they're talking about life. Adam's probably naming off a few invertebrates and the Lord presents Adam with His idea about supplying him with his new helper, his bride. The Bible obviously doesn't record every word so we're not sure if Adam was really sold on this new addition to the garden, or even if he understood everything God was about to do. He might have even been a little resistant about being put to sleep and losing a rib in order for this creation to be created, but make no mistake about

> *If there had ever been even the slightest question in his mind about if the Lord truly knew what He was doing in every situation that thought was totally obliterated when he first laid eyes on his new "help meet."*

it, when Adam woke up he was extremely pleased. If there had ever been even the slightest question in his mind about if the Lord truly knew what He was doing in every situation that thought was totally obliterated when he first laid eyes on his new "help meet."

I love what Adam said in Genesis 2:23-24:

The man said, "This is now bone of my bones and flesh of
my flesh; she shall be called 'woman,' for she was taken out
of man."

That is why a man leaves his father and mother and is united to
his wife, and they become one flesh.

Now, strip away the Kings English and the Shakespearean flavor
and I'm convinced that deeply rooted in the most ancient Hebrew
dialect and translation, somewhere in these two versus it really read
something like this, "Bam! That's what I'm talking about Yahweh!
Bye Mom and Dad. You bet I'm moving out of my room and out of
your house, and right now because we're gone! See you at Christmas
time. Don't smoke signal me, I'll smoke signal you! We'll send you
a post card!" And from that second on Adam searched every square
inch of that garden until he found a white sandy beach for his and
Eve's honeymoon!

Life was great and it would have stayed perfect if that's the way it
would have been lived from then until this very day, but it wasn't. It's
at this point in history where a major screw up is about to take place
and it's going to ultimately lead to the CEO of the world handing
over ownership to the enemy. And it's right here where we cut to the
chase and get to the core of our problem.

Listen closely. This is it! All our lives, from the time we see all
the drawings and hear all the stories of Adam and Eve we're taught it
was Eve who was deceived and sinned first. There is no doubt she was
deceived, but that wasn't the original sin so stop blaming her.

If Eve's conversation and eating the fruit was the first sin then why does the Word say in the New Testament that "by the sin of one man, sin entered the world"? Look at Romans 5:15-17:

> But the gift is not like the trespass. For if the many died by the trespass of the one man, how much more did God's grace and the gift that came by the grace of the one man, Jesus Christ, overflow to the many! Nor can the gift of God be compared with the result of one man's sin: The judgment followed one sin and brought condemnation, but the gift followed many trespasses and brought justification. For if, by the trespass of the one man, death reigned through that one man, how much more will those who receive God's abundant provision of grace and of the gift of righteousness reign in life through the one man, Jesus Christ!

Look at all three verses. It clearly talks about the trespass, but it's the sin of the one man, not the woman. If Eve's sin is the first that caused the entire fall of man then don't you think God would have said, "because of the sin of the one woman"? But He doesn't because He can't. Because that wouldn't be truth. It was the man.

So what was the sin? It's the same one the referee in the commercial committed and it's the same one you and I commit far too often. It's what I call the sin of passive, silent neglect. I know that's three words but I'm not omnipotent like God and I can't condense something so heinous into one word. But you can bet your destiny they all fit together, and like three dominoes standing all in a row, the fall of one leads to the fall of the rest. Here's the proof. In Genesis 3:1-7 we see

the conversation unfold between Eve and the serpent and the longer
it goes the uglier it gets. Look at it:

> Now the serpent was craftier than any of the wild animals the
> Lord God had made. He said to the woman, "Did God really
> say, 'You must not eat from any tree in the garden'?"
>
> The woman said to the serpent, "We may eat fruit from
> the trees in the garden, but God did say, 'you must not eat
> fruit from the tree that is in the middle of the garden, and
> you must not touch it, or you will die.'"
>
> "You will not certainly die," the serpent said to the
> woman. "For God knows that when you eat from it your
> eyes will be opened, and you will be like God, knowing good
> and evil."
>
> When the woman saw that the fruit of the tree was good
> for food and pleasing to the eye, and also desirable for gaining
> wisdom, she took some and ate it. She also gave some to
> her husband, who was with her, and he ate it. Then the eyes
> of both of them were opened, and they realized they were
> naked; so they sewed fig leaves together and made coverings
> for themselves.

In these 7 verses everything changed. A great man acted like a
wimp. A beautiful wife stepped out of her role. Cosmic ownership
and authority changed hands, mankind fell from a perfect relationship
and a pristine world became instantaneously cursed. But don't be
deceived another minute. It wasn't because the woman ate a piece of
fruit. It's because the man, the great champion, the hero, the CEO
of the world, stood there with his wife shoulder to shoulder...silent.

Look at it in verse 6. "she took some and ate it. She also gave some to her husband, *who was with her,* and he ate it."

Here we have the first lady of the world playing "chatty Cathy" with the devil and her husband, the one who is supposed to protect her, to watch over her, to pamper her and keep her from evil is just standing there while his wife is being verbally assaulted by the ultimate enemy and he says and does nothing! It would be like some man abusing your wife right in front of your eyes and you just stand there and allow it to happen, all the while having the power to stop it! Wake up Adam. Pull your head out from the sand or a rock or wherever you had it. Stand up, be a man, stop the abuse and run this serpent out of the garden and out of your lives forever!

My family and I were camping one time and our son Ryan and I were hiking. It was a trail we had been on countless times, and to get on the trail we had to cross a dry creek bed. Before we started, aloud I began claiming Psalms 91 for our protection and as I came to the part where it says, "We tread upon the lion and the serpent. We trample the great lion and the cobra." Ryan is kind of like, "uh, dad really?" And right after I finished claiming that portion I looked down in mid-stride, meaning my right foot is just about to touch the rocky creek bed, and about 12 inches below my foot lying square in my landing spot is a 3 foot long copperhead. For those of you who know anything about copperheads you'll know that one around 3 feet long is huge. It must have been an angel that intervened, because somehow in mid-air my right foot defied all gravitational forces and I was able to find traction and jump completely over the snake while at the same time pushing Ryan out of harms way. It was an Indiana Jones-like moment!

Now, for all you conservational type people, you're not going to like the next thing I did. But I found a rock about the size as the state of Texas and Ryan and I smashed that serpent's head so no one; man, woman, or child would ever be bitten by this snake. And no, we didn't lose one ounce of sleep knowing we had subtracted one copperhead from the animal kingdom that day. It's a dangerous snake. It was lying where tons of people, were going to be walking all day long and I wasn't going to just politely shoo it off into the bushes. I killed it. Dead! Done! No more risk from that reptile and that's exactly what Adam should have done to that serpent!

It's attacking your wife Adam. It's injecting poisonous venom into her leg Adam. It's killing her Adam. With demonic, evil eyes and a satanic smirk it's laughing at the situation, but it's specifically laughing at you Adam because it knows what's happening and you are just standing there cowardly watching. Adam, you have (had) all authority. You could have just told the serpent to shut up or better yet you could have taken a rock that was right by your foot and smashed his little head into the next life…but you just stood there. Watching. Listening. Doing nothing…and then participating in the destruction.

And here we are.

I'm totally convinced the original sin occurred well before this incident. In chapter 2 God told Adam, "You are free to eat from any tree in the garden; but you must not eat from the tree of the knowledge of good and evil, for when you eat from it you will certainly die." But in the conversation Eve was having with the enemy she tries to quote the command Adam received but said it this way, "We may eat fruit from the trees in the garden, but God did say, 'You must not eat fruit from the tree that is in the middle of the garden, *and you must not touch it,* or you will die." Where did the part, "and you must not touch it" come from? It wasn't in the original conversation between God and Adam so either Adam was a poor communicator, and that answers a lot of questions about most of us as guys, or Eve just added her two cents to a previous conversation between two other individuals, and that too answers a lot questions about problems in marriages as well. Either way, I believe the conversation with the serpent was simply life as it had become for the first couple. For some reason Adam chose to be passive which led to silence, which led to his dereliction of duty, which led to destruction.

Get this. This is serious. This is not a fairy tale. These are not just words in a book. This is where it all fell apart. This is where sin stepped in. This is where hell showed up. This is where selfishness and divorce were born. This is where the silence and passive neglect of men started and from that time on this beautiful,

> *This is where sin stepped in. This is where hell showed up. This is where selfishness and divorce were born.*

passionate life event between and man and a woman called marriage got screwed up. To this day as the result of his sin, both men and women enter into a covenant relationship with each other already in a dysfunctional state because it's been modeled that way for us ever since the beginning.

Come on Superman, where did you go? Why did you cave? Why did you put back on those clumsy clothes and goofy glasses? Why did you become silent? Why did you just stand there silently watching, letting it all fall apart? Why did you just hand over all the power and authority that had been given to you? Why did you relinquish your role as the voice and the hand of God?

Since that time it's been a mess. Just as we have no control over the DNA that is passed down to us from our parents, neither do we have control of the legacy that we received from Adam and Eve. It's all been screwed up ever since. But it doesn't have to stay that way any longer. That's why this is being written. It's to start a wake up call to all men around the world.

One last thing about silencing serpents. Look at the difference in the way Eve handled the temptation of the serpent in the Garden and how the Son of God handled it in the wilderness. Compare the two. Eve had a casual conversation with it like she was having a cup of coffee with an old friend. And she started her conversation with the word "we." In other words she was making the issue about herself… her self. And the more she talked the more entangled she became with the logic of the serpent.

Compare that to Jesus' dialogue with the enemy in the wilderness. The serpent presented his case to Jesus with the same order and structure he did with Eve, namely trying to question the words of God and build doubt from logic and what did Jesus do? What was the first word that left His mouth…It! He said, "It is written." In other words His defense was His offense. Jesus always answered the enemy with the Word! "It is written." "It is written."

With Eve it was flesh and self, "We may do this and we may do that." She made it about them. But Jesus always made it about the Word. He answered with the Word and men, it's the exact same way we are to answer the tempter today…with the Word.

Finally Jesus had enough of this serpent wasting His time and He simply told him to shut up and he did. It worked for Him then and it will work for us today, if you know the One who gives ultimate authority to His family.

Are you standing silently just watching destruction grip your home, or are you leading the battle of ridding your family of the enemy that seek to take it over? Remember, there is a battle going on! Nothing is ever won by passivity. The "quiet game" should only be played by first graders. And neglect will never lead to a Song of Songs honeymoon.

> Nothing is ever won by passivity. The "quiet game" should only be played by first graders.

Where are you Man of Standing? The enemy has been looking and he's located your home address and he's slithering your way. The next move is yours. Start looking for a Rock.

CHAPTER 4

SAVING OUR
OWN SKIN

I'm an intelligent guy. College graduate. I pride myself on being able to make the right decision most of the time. But there was one night when Liz and I were in our first couple of years of marriage that I just blew it. It was on that evening I had what I like to affectionately call a rectal-cranial inversion. Jim Moore translation...I had my head up my butt! Guys, do you know what it's like to be so enamored with something, like a sport, that you lose all wisdom and the ability to think rationally? There's something mysterious in all males, as if when we sleep on our sides too long half of our gray matter falls right out of our ears! That's where I was with my idolatrous relationship with Industrial League Softball.

Liz was pregnant and having some issues with the pregnancy. I on the other hand was a softball player with no issues being at

38

every game. You know this kind of league, all the men still trying to live in their glory days, who couldn't fit into their high school jerseys even if their lives depended on it. Men who just knew a scout from some major league team was scouring the country side hoping and praying to find the next Alex Rodriguez or Hank Aaron at a softball park! But I was serious. In fact so serious that before Liz and I married there was actually a summer when I played in over 80 games. It was so monumental to me that I carried this overrated, major league stud wanna-a-be attitude into our marriage. When she married me she married into my summer schedule for the sport. She was given no choice.

Now, for all you judgementalists out there let's settle this. Softball or any other recreational sport isn't a sin, unless you put it in front of God's name or your wife's needs. I did both.

Liz was starting to struggle a little with her first pregnancy. Some pain and spotting had begun so it was necessary for her to take it easy. The obvious and virtuous choice for me to make would have been to stay home, miss the game and attend to the needs of the one who before God I chose to love, honor, and cherish for the rest of our lives together. Guess which choice I made? You got it, I chose the stupid choice.

I looked at it like this: it wasn't life or death, and if Liz really felt like I needed to stay home she would have told me. It shouldn't have had to go there. Priorities men. I should have stayed home to be sure she was alright. It's called a foot rub. A back massage. A peaceful conversation that would lead to laughter as we planned out our dreams together. I chose option B. I left and something happened. The pain got worse and so did the spotting and I wasn't there. I was busy taking care of me.

I can't remember the score of the game. I can't remember if I got a hit. I can't even remember if we won, but here's what I can remember. I remember when I pulled my pickup truck into our driveway that her parent's car was already there. I remember that Liz was hurting more, spotting more, and feeling worse. I clearly remember the look I received

If looks could kill this God fearing deacon would have spent the rest of his life on death row.

from my father-in-law when he had the chance to catch eye contact with me when no one else was looking. No words were exchanged. Trust me, they didn't have to be. If looks could kill this God fearing deacon would have spent the rest of his life on death row.

It's been over 25 years since then and I still struggle with why something as insignificant as a softball game was chosen over someone that is supposed to be the priority of my life. I've thought about my moronic act countless times and I've come to a simple conclusion. I was selfish. Period! I wish I had a better answer. I wish I had one that would cause great debates between brilliant sociologists. An answer where books could be written and papers published that could help me feel better about my choice. But those answers didn't come. It came down to one word...selfish.

It was all about me. I couldn't miss a game! I was the coach. I bat clean up. I play second base. No one turns a double play like I can. My team needed me...but my wife needed me more. It was my own choice to put my self-centered, egocentric desires above her needs. Hers were real. Mine were superficial. Hers were about her health and our baby. Mine were about my enjoyment and a boy's night out. Bottom line, I was saving my own skin!

Now, before all you perfect husbands get your pile of rocks out to start stoning you need to look at your own track record. Whether you've been married 5 months or 50 years, chances are you've have created your own scrapbook and you've collected your own trophies, all at the cost of your wife. This "saving our own skin" has been perfectly modeled to us for generations. Possibly from dads or granddads, definitely from movie stars and sports figures. It is modeled by men all over the world. It seems everywhere you turn men are placing their most treasured possession on the back burner all in the name of putting their own needs and desires first. As a matter of fact, one of the greatest men in history pulled his own bonehead move that crushed the soul of his wife causing a tremendous amount of pain.

In the second century, Abraham, the father of our faith had just arrived onto the scene. He had been a pagan worshiper in the Ur of the Chaldeans with his family, but God had a plan. He chose Abraham to leave his place of idol worship and go to the Land of Promise and worship the one, true God…and he did. Abraham was riding high with the promises that God had given him. His name was made great. Anyone who blessed him God would bless, and anyone foolish enough to curse him God would curse. To top it off, God said that all the people on earth would be blessed through him. It would seem that promises like that would be more than enough to keep Abraham in check and obedient, but something happened along the way that caused even Abraham to have his own rectal-cranial inversion. Read it here:

The LORD had said to Abram, "Go from your country, your people and your father's household to the land I will show you.

"I will make you into a great nation, and I will bless you; I will make your name great, and you will be a blessing. I will bless those who bless you, and whoever curses you I will curse; and all peoples on earth will be blessed through you."

So Abram went, as the LORD had told him; and Lot went with him. Abram was seventy-five years old when he set out from Harran. He took his wife Sarai, his nephew Lot, all the possessions they had accumulated and the people they had acquired in Harran, and they set out for the land of Canaan, and they arrived there.

Abram traveled through the land as far as the site of the great tree of Moreh at Shechem. At that time the Canaanites were in the land. The LORD appeared to Abram and said, "To your offspring I will give this land." So he built an altar there to the LORD, who had appeared to him.

From there he went on toward the hills east of Bethel and pitched his tent, with Bethel on the west and Ai on the east. There he built an altar to the LORD and called on the name of the LORD.

Then Abram set out and continued toward the Negev.

So far, so good. Then comes verse 10 and for whatever reason Abraham allows his common sense, his male ego…something, to take over and make a radically poor decision:

Now there was a famine in the land, and Abram went down to Egypt to live there for a while because the famine was severe. As he was about to enter Egypt, he said to his wife Sarai, "I know what a beautiful woman you are. When the Egyptians see you, they will say, 'This is his wife.' Then they will kill me but will let you live. Say you are my sister, so that

I will be treated well for your sake and my life will be spared because of you."

When Abram came to Egypt, the Egyptians saw that Sarai was a very beautiful woman. And when Pharaoh's officials saw her, they praised her to Pharaoh, and she was taken into his palace. He treated Abram well for her sake, and Abram acquired sheep and cattle, male and female donkeys, male and female servants, and camels.

In the blink of an eye, just like we have all done at one time or another he set aside his sense of virtue and valor. The Bible said a famine came on the land and Abraham for some unknown reason decides to go to Egypt. Who said, "Go to Egypt Abraham?" Did God? I believe it was the enemy of reason, of common sense. Was this same God who took him out of Pagan worship and led him all the way to a Promised Land now going to abandon him just because of a famine? Playing armchair quarterback it's easy to see that in the eyes of Abraham, Yahweh was just a little smaller in stature and less potent in power than a famine. This famine appeared bigger than God. Nowhere in this story did God ever come close to saying, "Now Abraham, you stay right here in the land I personally have chosen for you and enjoy. Travel border to border and enjoy. But if a famine hits then you must immediately run to pagan country because they will become your source." Never was that said.

Now, it's easy being brutal on a guy that's been dead for over 5000 years, but the truth is I've been exactly where Abraham was and did the same thing. I've looked at some of the tough times in my life and my reaction to them, and it was at the exact point where I caved that I determined the level, size, and of power of my God. And chances are, so have you.

Abraham's natural senses, what he could see and then rationalize told him to go to man made cities where he and Sarah would be safe. There was just one problem. Sarah was gorgeous. Even for a 65 year old woman she carried such beauty that Abraham knew what would happen. So as he travels down this slippery slope to man made protection and provision, he continues his skin saving syndrome by asking the ultimate sacrifice of his wife. He even tried to mask it as being for her sake.

Look at verse 11: As he was about to enter Egypt, he said to his wife Sarai, "I know what a beautiful woman you are. When the Egyptians see you, they will say, 'This is his wife.' Then they will kill me but will let you live. Say you are my sister, so that I will be treated well *for your sake* and my life will be spared because of you."

Say what? You want to me to…what? Yeah, here's the real life, cut to the quick translation. Sarah, I could lose my life because of your beauty. So lie for me and tell them you're my sister. You're going to end up as one of Pharaoh's play things, but me…I'm going to come out of this thing smelling like a rose. This is going to crush you, but don't worry about me baby doll, I'm going to be just fine.

Stop. Let's camp here a while. Think about what just happened. Close the book for a few moments and let the choice that Abraham just made really sink in. This is not some fable or fairy tale. It happened, but there will be no stones cast from this pen. Each of us who have been married for any decent length of time have our own story of a time that for whatever reason we saved our skin at the price of our wife. Probably none of us have ever literally traded over our wives and their souls to slavery for our material good, but most if not all of us have tossed our wives and their tender needs aside for our selfishness. What have you lost? What loss did you bring on your wife?

Who knows what all happened in Pharaoh's house. We can only imagine, and I'm not going to linger on it, but by the grace of God a plague came over the house of Pharaoh, and it was determined that it was because there was a married woman among his group. Once they found out it was Sarah, she along with Abraham were quickly banished from Egypt, but not before Abraham, an already wealthy man, got much wealthier.

He treated Abram well *for her sake*, and Abram acquired sheep and cattle, male and female donkeys, male and female servants, and camels.

But the Lord inflicted serious diseases on Pharaoh and his household because of Abram's wife Sarai. So Pharaoh summoned Abram. "What have you done to me?" he said. "Why didn't you tell me she was your wife? Why did you say, 'She is my sister,' so that I took her to be my wife? Now then, here is your wife. Take her and go!" Then Pharaoh gave orders about Abram to his men, and they sent him on his way, with his wife and everything he had.

"Wow! We barely made it out alive, didn't we honey? Can you believe how mad Pharaoh was? For a while I really thought it was going to cost us something, but we made it out just fine…and look, we've got all these new shiny animals and servants and all this cool stuff! Our balance sheet just got a lot larger too. Now we're richer than ever. Hey I've got an idea, let's go back to the Promise Land and we can now really enjoy the good life!"

Or maybe it was complete silence as Abraham, with all his newly acquired treasure traveled silently as his wife crouched in a fetal position taking only shallow breaths, weeping uncontrollably in torment saying nothing at all. His net worth increased but Sarah's self worth was crushed. And every once in a while, with whatever little

His net worth increased but Sarah's self worth was crushed. And every once in a while, with whatever little amount of courage he could muster Abraham would cast his eyes in her direction to see if she was moving, and could only agonize and cry out on the inside of his tormented self asking, "What did I just do?"

amount of courage he could muster Abraham would cast his eyes in her direction to see if she was moving, and could only agonize and cry out on the inside of his tormented self asking, "What did I just do?"

This is an ugly chapter. I hate it. I wish that it didn't have to be written. But as a real man… as a Man of Standing, we must immediately wake up from our slumber of self-centeredness that causes damage to our wives as they too find themselves in fetal positions hoping that someday we'll realize that the one we said we'd love, honor, and cherish is still waiting for those words to come true. I know we say we love, cherish, and honor them as if we really know what that means. Every guy thinks he knows what love is, but unless the word "sacrificial" is inserted before the word love, we really have no concept of it. None! And you can forget about honor and cherishing. But that's what she expects and that's what she deserves. They deserve our all. They deserve our absolute best! The problem is most of us as guys don't even know the power we possess (if you know the Ultimate King of All Power) to make it all happen.

I wonder what must have gone through Sarah's mind every time she looked out the kitchen window into the pastures and saw all the livestock that Abraham possessed because she herself was once a possession too. Probably similar to the way Liz might have felt when she was spotting and cramping as she watched the one who before God promised to love, honor, and cherish her drive away to his boys night out. How about you? What goes through your wife's mind when she looks at the golf clubs, the boat, the cars, the animal heads hanging on the wall, every sporting event on TV, the unending business travel...all the stuff that you've acquired at the cost *for her sake?*

Is all this stuff bad? Absolutely not. As a matter of fact I'm totally convinced God wants His children to possess enjoyable things, as long as they don't possess us, and as long as they are instruments that strengthen a marriage and family and not divide it. Boats, cars, and sporting events are awesome but so is shopping, lunch dates with her, and back rubs without expecting anything in return. Anything that meets the delicate needs of her soul that she longs for from you.

On another occasion that I had the opportunity to be sitting in the right seat on a corporate jet with an incredible pilot and fight instructor. While we were on the runway he was busy programming the flight computer so that after takeoff and at a certain altitude, he could flip the little red button and the flight computer would take over. He delicately programmed all the data parameters with careful precision knowing just one wrong number could have us going in the wrong direction.

Once our flight plan was loaded into the computer he switched on the engines, received clearance from the tower, taxied to the end of the runway, set the flaps, pushed down on the throttle, screamed down the runway, pulled back on the wheel and away we went... headed back home.

We had just broken over the clouds and passed 20,000 feet when I looked over at him and told him that I just had to learn to fly. Without batting an eye he said, "Grab the wheel." Once I had done so he flipped off the automatic pilot and there I was, climbing towards 25,000 feet above the clouds at over 300 miles per hour! Let me be brutally honest at this point, my pucker factor was at an all time tightness. I love driving 75 miles an hour on a flat 8 lane interstate, but this was far from that scenario. With a James Bond-like calmness in his voice he said, "5 degrees to the left." I acted like I knew what I was doing so I just ever so slightly moved the wheel in that direction. Then he instructed me to keep my eyes on the levelizer gauge so I would keep the craft on the right plane. I only flew for about 5 minutes but it seemed like 5 hours even with his hands on the other steering wheel. By now I'm covered from head to toe in sweat...at least I hoped that's what it was in my pants!

I looked at the pilot and said that I was ready for him to take back over the wheel and so he did. He pushed the little red button that put the jet back on automatic pilot and immediately the jet took a sharp turn to the starboard side. I looked at him and said "What just happened?" Now you've got to know this guy to fully appreciate his next comment. He's got over 12,000 hours of flight time and he's as cool as a cucumber. He just looked at me through his aviator sunglasses with a big smile and said, "We just got back on course." He said the wind and other circumstances can blow you off course fairly easily, and ever so subtly that you'd never even know it was doing so. When you put it back on autopilot, it gets you back to the place you're supposed to be.

That's when God Almighty showed up in the cockpit of that Cessna Citation. He showed me that it is exactly like my life. Before I ever took off and was born on this planet, He programmed my steps from point A to point Z. With great precision and an indescribable love for me He planned a journey that would be greater than anything I could ask or imagine. He traveled into my future not planning hardships and trouble, but instead mapping out a course that would keep me from it. But somewhere along the flight I took back control by taking it out of His hands and putting it into my own. I started watching the circumstances of life and calling them truth. I mastered the system of this world and called it the Kingdom of God, and I let myself be pushed around by turbulent circumstances that blew me off course. But when I turned the controls of my life back over to Him, He simply turned the vessel back in the intended direction. And that's what this book is about. It's about looking at where we all find ourselves and making the necessary changes that will get us, our marriage, and our families back to our intended destination. Some turns are going to be subtle and some are going to be an uncomfortable, maybe even a full 180 degrees. It all depends on where you start. Some might think that any turn would be unnecessary and some of you might think it's impossible to get back on track with all that has happened in your life. Wherever you are, God is the God of another chance. His story of unspeakable love, incomprehensible mercy, and unimaginable redemption is greater than any failure and He's waiting on you to trust Him again give Him the controls. Starting might be radical and hard, but start you must.

There was probably no easy answer for Abraham and Sarah to get back on track with one another. It took God's anointing, His healing, and probably some time to pass to heal the scars. It's probably going to take the same for us today.

Men, make it a priority today to stop allowing your actions or lack thereof being the source of pain in your wife's life, and start to

Men, make it a priority today to stop allowing your actions or lack thereof being the source of pain in your wife's life, and start to become a source of life for her.

become a source of life for her. Women just want the pain to stop and will sometimes go to great lengths to make that happen, and many times those can lead straight toward a wrong path.

In every place of pain in Ruth's life, Boaz and his actions became a source of healing and so too should our lives and actions be for our own wife and family.

Where are you? Are you lost in your own self-centered world with little to no regard of the most precious person you've been given, or are you totally committed to being everything you told her you would be when you said, "I do"?

It's time to put your life and your marriage back into the control of the One who designed it in the first place. He's the One who can fix it. Don't keep her another day in slavery. She's been waiting long enough.

CHAPTER 5

BOAZ, THE TRUE MAN OF STANDING

The day he showed up, everything changed. Testosterone flowed through the streets. When this man among boys came on to the scene dreams became reality, wrongs were made right and romance got real. I can clearly see it. His appearance alone commands attention when he shows up, and everyone stops and stares because there is no doubt in anyone's mind who this man is. His powerful reputation precedes him. His profitable actions back it up. This guy is a stud. Every man there dreams they could be him, and every woman present checks to make sure she suddenly looks her very best. As this hero looks over the crowd that is undoubtedly looking at him he sees one particular woman. And the moment he sees her he knows he must have her. In a few moments she will be speechless. In a few moments she will be breathless. With absolute confidence while exploding in virtue he goes straight to her, and the second he opens his mouth and speaks both their direction and their destiny change forever.

I'm a guy. I can't stand cheesy romance novels. They take up too much room in a book store, and they have the same guy on every cover with just a different hairdo striking the same worn out pose. You've seen it. Wearing a shirt that looks like a cross between something a pirate and a disco dancer would wear. He is leaning over her, steamily gazing into the eyes of the woman of his dreams, her blouse half unbuttoned, her hair flowing in the wind, holding her in his arms *at a 45 degree angle*. Of course it's not real because no real man would be caught dead in that shirt or that pose. But this story is different. The one you just read is real and it can cause your male hormone levels to go off the charts. No, it's not Superman and Lois. It's Boaz and Ruth!

Here it is men. It's perfectly laid out for us to seize, and if we unlock this mystery we too can taste the sweet fruits that this mystifying relationship called marriage is supposed to be like. Today, make a conscious decision to immediately leave the desert that has led to a journey of mediocrity and failure and begin to walk fully into the promise land of strength and oneness. It's time for this lifeless, loveless, dysfunctional relationship with your spouse to be healed and to be put in its proper place. We've been desperately searching for answers and instructions since the day we said "I do," and ironically it's been openly displayed yet waiting to be discovered in one of the least sought out places you'd think. The real manual for real manhood...the Bible.

Here is the story. We find it in the Book of Ruth in the Old Testament. Chapter 1 tells us about a woman named Ruth who had lost virtually everything. She had lost her husband and all that died with him. Their dreams and plans. Their hopes. Everything they had worked for, gone. All that was left was a gaping hole in her soul. Couple that tragic loss with the fact the she was now moving to the homeland of her mother-in-law. The problem with this relocation was that Ruth was a Moabite and she was going to live in the Land of Judah. To you and I, this is no more than a glossed over fact, but in those days in the eyes of an Israelite, Moabites were a notch above pond scum.

They were descendants of Moab, son of Lot. Lot, nephew to Abraham, had raised his family in the towns of Sodom and Gomorrah, an absolute toxic dump of every deviant sexual sin imaginable. A region where if 10 righteous people could have been found, it would not have been destroyed by God Almighty. An area where such vile acts not worthy of taking the time to write on these pages were committed on a daily basis, yet a town where Lot, for whatever reason thought he could raise his family.

One night three angels came to Lot and told him to leave because God was getting ready to level this unrepentant region. Believe it or not, because he and his family had driven their stakes so deep into that dirt these angels had to literally drag them out of there. You can read the story in Genesis 19. Read it on an empty stomach, it's nauseating. That night Lot also lost his wife, because as they was being rescued from judgment, she just had to take one more over the shoulder glimpse of her hometown, and she immediately perished into a pile of salt. So Lot found himself hiding and living in a cave with his two daughters, both virgins.

Because these girls had grown up in maggot-like filth at every corner, they logically reasoned between the two of them the only way they were ever going to bare children living in this cave was to get their father drunk, have sex with dad and conceive a child with him, and they did. Years of depraved behavior being modeled had come home to roost. Years of watching vile seeds be planted brought an equally vile harvest. Welcome Moab. And that's the reputation Ruth would carry back on her shoulders to her mother-in-law's country. A gigantic hole in her soul and an unholy heritage.

Now, before we go another inch in this love story, we've got to jump to chapter 3 of Ruth. Here we find the same hurting woman we saw in chapter 1 who now is literally putting on her hottest clothes, perfuming herself from head to toe, and pursuing her dream man. She secretly goes to where he's working and staying for the night. Not wanting to be seen, she sneaks in. She's secretly watching him work! She's checking out his muscles and she waits until he is "in good spirits!" Manhood translation, "a third glass of wine!" And once he lies down for the night she quietly slips over to him, uncovers a portion of his body, lies down beside him, and waits for him to tell her what to do. And no, this is not fiction!

Here is the million dollar question men. Answer it correctly, live it out fully and marriage can become so much sweeter. How did this broken down woman with a gigantic hole in her soul from all that had happened to her in chapter 1 find herself daringly and romantically pursuing this champion among men in chapter 3?

Answer: To go from chapter 1 to chapter 3 she had to travel through chapter 2. That's where everything changed. That's where the authentic manhood actions of Boaz collided with the genuine feminine needs of Ruth, and an explosion of passion took place

Quit settling for a tiny little spark between the two of you and thinking that's as good as it gets.

between the two of them. If you and I want to encounter marriage with all its beauty, passion, and oneness we too must take that journey through chapter 2. Quit settling for a tiny little spark between the two of you and thinking that's as good as it gets. Man up and start an explosion in your manhood. Raise the bar. Expand your possibilities and chapter 2 is where you'll find it. That's where it starts. Let the Creator of passion and oneness fill you to overflowing with His passion and His plan. Whether you're 21 or 91, stop wasting time, man up and let's get this done. It's our destiny. Better yet, it's God's destiny He designed for us, if you're brave enough to believe it and do something about it. Chapter 2 is where the treasure map is found and it's where we too must travel. And it's also where we must come to grips with the truth of where you are and where you can be. How bad do you want it? Want to be pursued by your wife? Then become pursuit worthy. Want to leave her breathless? Then change the way you breathe. Now, before we dive into this love story let me make one thing clear. It's my opinion that Boaz found an immediate attraction for Ruth. You might have Hebrew scholars that don't read that into the story at first, but from my standpoint I think he was hooked from the second he laid eyes on her. Look at chapter 2:

Now Naomi had a relative on her husband's side, a man of standing from the clan of Elimelek, whose name was Boaz.

And Ruth the Moabite said to Naomi, "Let me go to the fields and pick up the leftover grain behind anyone in whose eyes I find favor."

Naomi said to her, "Go ahead, my daughter." So she went out, entered a field and began to glean behind the harvesters.

As it turned out, she was working in a field belonging to Boaz, who was from the clan of Elimelek.

Just then Boaz arrived from Bethlehem and greeted the harvesters, "The LORD be with you!"

"The LORD bless you!" they answered.

Boaz asked the overseer of his harvesters, "Who does that young woman belong to?"

The overseer replied, "She is the Moabite who came back from Moab with Naomi. She said, 'Please let me glean and gather among the sheaves behind the harvesters.' She came into the field and has remained here from morning till now, except for a short rest in the shelter."

So Boaz said to Ruth, "My daughter, listen to me. Don't go and glean in another field and don't go away from here. Stay here with the women who work for me. Watch the field where the men are harvesting, and follow along after the women. I have told the men not to lay a hand on you. And whenever you are thirsty, go and get a drink from the water jars the men have filled."

At this, she bowed down with her face to the ground. She asked him, "Why have I found such favor in your eyes that you notice me—a foreigner?"

Sound like your house? Here's the picture. Ruth needed to work to eat and as it turned out she found herself in the right field at the right time to meet Boaz, the "man of standing". Again, the word "standing" in Hebrew means a "force of men, means, resources, wealth, virtue, valor, strength and able," and the word "man" in this instance means "champion or mighty".

Put the two together and here's what you get. A mighty man of force. A might man of means. A mighty man of resources. A mighty man of wealth. A mighty man of strength. A champion of virtue. A champion of valor. A champion that is able! There it is, the true definition of manhood. What our wives secretly want and what the world desperately needs. That's how the God of the universe designed it and it's up to you and me to believe it and accept it. Boaz received it and so can you. He walked it out and it paid great dividends to him and his legacy. This can be you too. This journey of "standing" was created to be used for your good and for the good of the world, and what you have in your hands is the roadmap to secure it…if you want it badly enough.

How incredible could life become if when your wife thinks of you or when she speaks about you to her friends, that this is how she describes you? That there would be no complaining, or concerns, or lack of confidence in you. That this definition of a real man is the mental image that pops into her mind. That just the thought of you can cause her heart to pound and her palms to sweat. That she's checking you out when you step out of the shower. Too tough you say? Sound a little worldly? We've got to get honest with ourselves men. No one is pushing us to become this champion. Mediocrity is the new standard. Estrogen is the new male hormone and nice guys are the new model. Almost everything is leading us to be uninspiring, unexciting, and boring guys that daily forfeit our masculinity. But that's not the way we were created. We were meticulously designed and crafted by the hand of God to be strong and courageous. To be fearless and to

That just the thought of you can cause her heart to pound and her palms to sweat. That she's checking you out when you step out of the shower.

lead. To have a backbone of steel and should some giant in life be foolish enough to stand in our way, we tell it what we're about to do to it just as David did to Goliath, and then we move it out of our way by the power of the Most High God. It's in you if you know the One who crafted and created you and it's right here that a decision has to be made. Do you stay in the deadly quicksand we all find ourselves in at one time or another, or do you lift up your eyes and realize there is a life of "standing" waiting on all of us who are daring and courageous enough to put it all on the line and see our destiny become reality. Answer this now. Would you rather leave each day for work with your wife feeling bored or breathless?

Now, for all you males out there who think that this Superman type of effort needed is an "anti-grace, self-help, new-age, Zen-like teaching," and you really don't believe in the importance of creating this type of urgency and obsession about working on your manhood, then you need to stop hitting the snooze button, rip the lace off your underwear, and wake up to the fact that what you reap will be what you sow. I am without question a grace person. I am totally sold to the truth that it is by grace alone that we receive a relationship with the Son of God. And I am completely committed that it is God's plan for us to receive His abundant gift of grace and His gift of righteousness in order that we might reign in life (Romans 5:17). And I believe it's totally by grace that we receive all this, but there is still a human response to a divine call. Want to have children? Then a seed must be planted. Want to have a rock hard body? Then a weight must be lifted. If your mentality is to do nothing then welcome to your reality! I'm not talking perfection. I'm talking about daily planting seeds of "standing" because that's what our wives thought they were getting when they married us. Answer this question: If your dating actions then were anything like your married actions now, would she have even said yes to a second date?

Sow little, reap little. But sow true manhood seeds that meets her greatest needs and people will line up to ask you how your marriage went from what they once saw to how it is now. Compare this incredible journey to that of a gold medal winner or a Super Bowl MVP. Haven't you ever dreamed what it would be like to stand on the podium having conquered that challenge? To be known as the best? For the very few of those who have, just ask them what it took to get there.

First, it took a vision of what it can be like, that led to a passion, that turned into a red-hot obsession. Add to that a roadmap or plan, and a relentless commitment to the plan. It took faith and unwavering courage to daily execute that plan even when everyone else had long quit for the day. It took determination and perseverance so that even when all those dark hours appeared (and they will) there was no option but to stay in and see the dream become a reality. That's where nothing but praise and worship to the One who can make it happen comes into play. That's the same degree of passion you will need for this journey. If that's what you want. And if it's not what you want then my friend you need to wake up because you're missing the show. This is what you were made for. This is the dance! Not every man can be Hall of Fame sports heroes but all of us can be Hall of Fame super husbands! The good news is everything you need, every tool and every answer for the race can be found in a deep love relationship with God, His Son, and His Spirit!

Boaz was a force. A force moves mountains. A force clears a path. A force is great influence. A force changes destinies. A force is also a super magnetic. A force changes the world and a virtuous force can draw your wife to you like you've never imagined. He was a force among men. He was a leader. A business owner. Men respected and looked up to him. Look at how he spoke to his harvesters. As he rode in and surveyed his fields being worked he reached out to his employees and said, "The Lord be with you!" Today if we even utter a "God bless you" to some people, even in the church they look at us like we're some charismatic wacko. Boaz on the other hand blessed his employees and his employees blessed him back.

What type of harvest could you have in your marriage if you daily planted seeds of verbal blessings into your wife? Not hatred, bitter seeds, or the typical "I'm tired after a hard day's work so leave me alone type seed." But seeds that lift her up. Seeds that restore her soul. Seeds that empower her. Seeds that bring out her inner and outer beauty. Seeds that heal and breathe life to her. "You're an incredible wife!" "You're absolutely beautiful inside and out!" "You're incredible!" "You deserve the best!" "You make my day complete!" Just to name a few. Boaz knew how to bless others and it paid huge dividends.

Boaz was a force of means. He must have been a man of considerable financial resources. To be a man of means denotes income, earnings, revenue, and capital. He created jobs. He created income for others. He created opportunity.

We presently live in a world that has experienced rapid changes pertaining to wealth and opportunity over the last few years, and in order for us as men to thrive we need to get serious with God in our approach to our income and our means. In spite of what you may have been taught, God does have a great plan for your family's finances and it's not poverty or lack. Now clearly hear what I'm about to say. I do not believe it to be the will of God for any man to succumb to a system that has you working ridiculous hours each week missing out on building your marriage, or spending priceless time away from your family all in the name of provision or planning for the future. There might be seasons of intense labor, but nowhere will you find God giving you permission to work in a system that creates a model of consistently losing time building your family. A Man of Standing is creative. With so many recent advances in technology there has never been this many opportunities of building multiple rivers of revenue through things like the internet or networking, and a Man of Standing will be that force that seeks the creator of all the gold and the owner of all the gold to show us where we can find it for our good and His glory. If the majority of marital stress comes from finance pressure, and I believe it does, then you must become intentional about being a force of means. The word doesn't say that "My God shall supply all your needs according to you working 60 hours a week," but it does say He'll supply it according to "His riches in glory." And He has a plan that will work for all of us, not just a select few. We've become so enamored with a Babylonian system that worships and idolizes men who create great wealth by working long, lost hours. If there is a little family carnage along the way then that's just how the ball bounced! That's just plain wrong.

Show me a man who has found the love of God to where it's radically, supernaturally changed his life. Show me a man who has discovered who he truly is in Christ and has received ALL the finished work that Christ accomplished on the cross for him. Show me a man who has discovered the true will of God for himself and his family, not some boring traditional, denominational way of life most call the will of God. Show me a man who had the guts to boldly approach the throne of God with confidence and take Him up on His words in Romans 5:17, that if we receive His abundance of grace and His gift of righteousness, then we'll reign in this life. Show me a man who has exploded out of this Babylonian box and created means for his family God's way. Show me a man who has the courageous faith to get out of the boat and start walking on water. Show me a man who spends more time with his wife and kids daily than he does in his labor. Show me a man who has found the measure of the fullness of God (Eph. 3:20) and leads his family and walks in it daily. Show me a man who was bold enough to ask God to create for him means and riches to bless his family financially, and who does good with it, and could care less what his family and friends thinks because his success doesn't look like the norm, and I'll show a man who has discovered the life and destiny of "standing".

We'd better get serious about discovering and living out this life of standing, and we need to get creative and bold and carry out a plan for multiple streams of revenues for our family. I attended a seminar where some of the greatest names in business, politics, sports, and entertainment spoke about living out a passionate and successful life. It was entertaining but the most informative and powerful speaker was a man I had never heard of. He was one of those fillers between the big names, but this guy kept everyone on the edge of their seats. He was hilarious yet had real substance. In the middle of his presentation he made a statement that I will never forget. He said, "If you don't have at least three streams of revenue coming into your business or household, that's insane." He went on to say that he currently had seven streams of income! What's your financial plan? God already has one in mind for you. Now, go find the courage to discover it and do it.

Boaz was a force of resources, meaning he had a collection of wealth and was a source of supply when the need arose. Similar words are those like wealth, property, possessions, funds, and wherewithal. A Man of Standing is just that. He is a river of resources that flows wealth and resources to those in need.

2 Corinthians 9 says that bountiful sowers reap a bountiful harvest. It says that our store of seed will be increased and the harvest of our righteousness will be enlarged. Then it says these words that so few people truly believe. "You will be made rich in every way that you may be generous on every occasion." Having the ability to meet financial needs at any given time is being a force of resources. What if you could write a million dollar check to a ministry that desperately needed it to rescue those from perishing? Think it's impossible? I'm sorry your god is too small.

Boaz was a mighty man of wealth. This is where I know I'm going to lose some religious people because here's the part about wealth and money. I was raised in a denomination that seldom overtly crossed the line to teach that having money was evil, but it sure walked up to it on many occasions. Everyone loved to preach against anyone pursuing money, but they sure loved those who had it when it came time to build a new building or buy a few buses. It wasn't until I stopped skating around issues and took off the religious blinders and began to literally believe the Word of God that I discovered what God had to say about His plan for creating wealth. So that there will be no question to my belief, here it is in print. God desires His children to be blessed, abundant and prosperous because that's what His Word says! Period!

Quit looking at your denominational teaching as if it is the ultimate source of all truth. Stop looking at someone's circumstances in life and

Quit looking at your denominational teaching as if it is the ultimate source of all truth. Stop looking at someone's circumstances in life and believing that this must be God's will for them!

believing that this must be God's will for them! Circumstances are facts not truth. The only pure truth is what comes from the mouth of God. So let examine just a few statements from God concerning wealth and prosperity, and note the words I have put in bold:

Remember the LORD your God. He is the one who gives you the ability to **create wealth** and **so fulfills His covenant he confirmed to your ancestors with an oath**. Deut. 8:18

All praise to God, the Father of our Lord Jesus Christ, **who has blessed us with every spiritual blessing** in the heavenly realms because we are united with Christ. Ephesians 1:3

Praise the LORD. Blessed are those who fear the LORD, who find great delight in his commands. Their children will be mighty in the land; the generation of the upright will be blessed. **Wealth and riches are in their houses, and their righteousness endures forever.** Psalms 112:1-3

With me are riches and honor, enduring wealth and prosperity. My fruit is better than fine gold; what I yield surpasses choice silver. I walk in the way of righteousness, along the paths of justice bestowing a rich inheritance on those who love me and making their treasuries full. Proverbs 8:18-21

The LORD be exalted, **who delights in the prosperity of his servant.** Psalms 35:27

The blessing of the Lord brings wealth, without painful toil for it. Proverbs 10:22

Your gates will always stand open. *They will never be shut day or night so that people may bring you the wealth of the nations.* Isaiah 60:11

Bring the whole tithe into the storehouse, that there may be food in my house. Test me in this," says the LORD Almighty, "*and see if I will not throw open the floodgates of heaven and pour out so much blessing that there will not be room enough to store it. I will prevent pests from devouring your crops, and the vines in your fields will not drop their fruit before it is ripe," says the* LORD *Almighty. "Then all the nations will call you blessed, for yours will be a delightful land," says the* LORD *Almighty* Malachi 3:10-12

Give, and it will be given to you. A good measure, pressed down, shaken together and running over, will be poured into your lap. For with the measure you use, it will be measured to you." Luke 6:38

A good person leaves an inheritance for their children's children, *but a sinner's wealth is stored up for the righteous.* Proverbs 13:22

For you know the grace of our Lord Jesus Christ, *that though he was rich, yet for your sake he became poor, so that you through his poverty might become rich.* 2 Cor. 8:9

Now he who supplies seed to the sower and bread for food will also supply and increase your store of seed and will enlarge the harvest of your righteousness. *You will be made rich in every way so that you can be generous on every occasion, and through us your generosity will result in thanksgiving to God.* 2 Cor 9:10, 11

May God be gracious to us and bless us and make his face shine on us—so that your ways may be known on earth, your salvation among all nations. May the peoples praise you, God; may all the peoples praise you. May the nations be glad and sing for joy, for you rule the peoples with equity and guide the nations of the earth. May the peoples praise you, God; may all the peoples praise you. The land yields its harvest; God, our God, blesses us. May God bless us still, so that all the ends of the earth will fear him. Psalm 67

For this reason I, Paul, the prisoner of Christ Jesus for the sake of you Gentiles— Surely you have heard about the administration of God's grace that was given to me for you, that is, the mystery made known to me by revelation, as I have already written briefly. In reading this, then, you will be able to understand my insight into the mystery of Christ, which was not made known to people in other generations as it has now been revealed by the Spirit to God's holy apostles and prophets. *This mystery is that through the gospel the Gentiles are heirs together with Israel, members together of one body, and sharers together in the promise in Christ Jesus.*

I became a servant of this gospel by the gift of God's grace given me through the working of his power. *Although I am less than the least of all the Lord's people, this grace was given me: to preach to the Gentiles the boundless riches of Christ*, Eph 3:1-8

I'm not going to take a lot of time to try and convince those of you who are still in disagreement, but what do you do with Deuteronomy 8:18 where it clearly says it is God's will to create wealth *and so confirms His covenant!* Or for you New Covenant people what do you do with 2 Corinthians 9? You will be made rich in every way so that you can be generous on any occasion! Quit listening to mere men as if they were God and begin to listen to the author of the very words many of you have chosen not to believe. Remember this. Anything that pushes you or takes you away from what God said is nothing more than an agenda. Someone, somewhere in history read a part of the Word about money and said, "It just can't be that good," and so created a way of thinking that was passed down for so long it became a theology. Remember the words of Christ in John 10:10, "I am come that you might have life and have it more abundantly." In Greek it is Perissos, meaning exceeding some number or measure or rank or need; over and above, more than is necessary, superadded, exceeding abundantly, supremely, superior, extraordinary, pre-eminence, superiority, advantage, more eminent, more remarkable, more excellent! Does that sound like you're life? We've diluted the Word with our religious agendas to the point that the truth becomes null and void. Boaz didn't do it and neither should you. By the way, there is a reason for wealth. There is a purpose for prosperity. There is so much that can be done with a large bank account and a willing heart. Ministries can be funded. Missionaries can be sent. The Word can go around the world. And yes, God gives it to us for our enjoyment too. He tells us in I Timothy 6:17. It is for our good and His glory. God wants us to possess things. Just don't let them possess you! Remember, seek His Kingdom first and then all these things will be added to us. I'm not saying that money and wealth are the key to a great marriage. But it's an incredibly important spoke on the wheel. Answer this: Is life easier or harder in poverty or financial lack? Financial struggles in marriage is like driving a car with two flat tires. You might ultimately get to where you're going but the ride is going to be rough and the damage to the vehicle will take its toll. Boaz, without question, was a force of wealth! Let's become one too.

Boaz was a force of virtue! Moral excellence. You won't find any cat calls or jokes coming from Boaz to the other harvesters as he looked and inquired about Ruth. No coarse jokes about Ruth's body. No junior high locker room giggles comes from this man's mouth. Nothing but virtuous comments. Nothing but valiant actions. As a matter of fact, when the harvester was describing her to Boaz he played the Moabite card and he received absolutely no response from his boss. On the contrary, Boaz went straight to Ruth and began to immediately change her life.

Boaz was a champion of valor. Heroic courage. Boldness. Bravery. This might clear it up. The opposite meaning is cowardice. Boaz was a champion of bravery who didn't back down in the face of adversity. He didn't shy away when things got a little rough and didn't run and hide when challenges came his way. He could have easily rolled with the tide of public opinion about the Moabite and worried about his reputation, but he loved what he saw and nothing, not a biased heritage or anything else was going to keep him from pursuing and captivating the woman of his desires.

Boaz was a champion of strength. He was obviously strong financially and in resources. But strength can take on many forms such as intellectual, financial, and physical. The latter is the direction I'm going to take. Boaz was somewhat older than Ruth although we don't know by how much, but there was still a physical appearance to him that definitely caught the eye of Ruth and caused her to literally stalk him in chapter 3. Now let's carefully cover the disclaimer about physical strength and conditioning. There will be those who adopt the Man of Standing vow who aren't presently or may never be capable of working on their physical strength because of an injury or some other physical type of setback they have endured. I've got a good friend that is a quadriplegic from a horrific fall from a ladder during a Christmas who is more of a Man of Standing than most men I know. You don't have to look like a muscle magazine cover. But for the vast majority of those who are capable of physical conditioning, this section is definitely for you.

The bottom line to being a force of strength is this. If you're capable of shaping your body into something that would be extremely pleasing to your wife, then get off your butt, join a gym, invest in an exercise program, and turn your body into something that would cause her to turn hers to you. Men today have adopted a double standard. We want our wives in shape and at their absolute best, but are we willing to pay the price and lead the way in this area? Think about what she'd like for you to look like and determine to make it happen.

A note for people who say that "beauty is fleeting and exercise profits little." Keep it in context. I am not saying you should allow your body to become your god but there is nothing, absolutely nothing wrong with wanting to look the absolute best for your wife. I guarantee, once you get there she's not going to complain. By the way, look what God says in the book of Song of Songs, chapter 5 about how the young maiden is dripping with love as she describes her man:

My beloved is radiant and ruddy, outstanding among ten
  thousand.
His head is purest gold; his hair is wavy and black as a raven.
His eyes are like doves by the water streams, washed in milk,
  mounted like jewels.
His cheeks are like beds of spice yielding perfume.
His lips are like lilies dripping with myrrh.
His arms are rods of gold set with topaz.
His body is like polished ivory decorated with sapphires.
His legs are pillars of marble set on bases of pure gold.
His appearance is like Lebanon, choice as its cedars.
His mouth is sweetness itself; he is altogether lovely.
This is my beloved, this is my friend.

Any questions? 10,000 men show up and 9,999 go home
disappointed because there was one who chose to be a Man of
Standing. Arms like rods of gold. A body like polished ivory. Sounds
like she'd love for you to have a 6 pack. And I'm talking about
abdominal muscles not beer. There's your challenge. There's your
goal. Look like that and see what kind of welcome you can receive
at the door.

There are too many men in the world who want their wives to
look like a cross between a *Baywatch* model and a female gymnast,
yet who won't lift a finger—much less a weight—to get themselves
in better physical condition. That's not a Man of Standing. That's
a sloth of sitting. Get a check up and get going. Set a goal. Find a
picture of what you want to look like and make it happen. I'll say
it one more time. Pay the price. Get in shape. Find out that the
label "chiseled" looks best attached to your body instead of a Greek

statue, and enjoy the benefits of your hard work with your wife. One last word about the physical. A true Man of Standing carries with him all the attributes of Superman. Although this hero could stop a freight train and then lift it over his head, you never heard him bragging about his strength like a boastful Neanderthal, and you never caught Superman flexing in front of Lois Lane to feed his flesh. Those men who only focus on the outward are superficial and shallow. Their actions are all about themselves and never for the other person. Men of Standing are not primadonnas who can't see past a mirror because manhood is produced from within. True manhood comes from within and permeates itself outward through inner love, a peaceful heart, a heart at rest knowing what God says about you. It starts on the inside and grows out and women catch that security in a Man of Standing and they want to connect with that person in a meaningful way. Our wives want and deserve the total package. Be that man!

Boaz was a man who was able! I love this attribute. How fantastic would it be for someone to ask your wife, "Is your husband able to (fill in the blank)?" and she says, "Well of course he can!" Being able is having the power needed. The intellect needed. The skill set needed. The knowledge needed. The guts needed. It's not being Albert Einstein or any other super brain. It's simply being a man who is able to get the job done, either doing it himself, figuring it out if he can't, or at least being able to hire it out. It's getting the job done. Period! The opposite...incompetence. Which one are you? Choose your legacy men.

Here's the incredible thing. This might not be what she is able to perfectly say about you today, but it can be what she sees and what she says about you tomorrow and the choice is up to you. Choose this day what the rest of your life will be like. You have a free will given to you by your creator. Use that freedom to become her dream.

The day he showed up, everything changed. Testosterone flowed through the streets. When this man among boys came on to the scene dreams became reality, wrongs were made right and romance got real. I can clearly see it. His appearance alone commands attention when he shows up and everyone stops and stares because there is no doubt in anyone's mind who this man is. His powerful reputation precedes him. His profitable actions back it up. This guy is a stud. Every man there dreams they could be him and every woman present checks to make sure she suddenly looks her very best. As this hero looks over the crowd that is undoubtedly looking at him he sees one particular woman. And the moment he sees her he knows he must have her. In a few moments she will be speechless. In a few moments she will be breathless. With absolute confidence yet not lacking in virtue he goes straight to her and the split second he opens his mouth and speaks both their direction and their destiny change forever.

May that be said about you and your wife? May that be said about all of us? May that be said about all real men. Make it happen right now.

CHAPTER 6

THE ULTIMATE MAGNETIC FORCE

It seems like I've rewritten the opening paragraph to this chapter at least 55 times because the truths in this section are so important for our success that I can't find the words forceful enough to describe it. Each time I rewrite them they come across more poetic than powerful so I'm scrapping 383 words and I'm cutting to the chase.

What you're about to read literally caused Ruth, in a matter of a few moments, to fall head over heels for a man she had just met. Not just any man, he was THE man, and it wasn't love at her first sight. It became love at his first might and as testosterone flowing XY chromosome filled creatures this is the stuff that causes our juices to flow and victories in our marriages to soar. This is serious stuff. This is for the men who want to be real. This is for men who want to put back on that Superman cape and courageously wear it without an ounce of embarrassment or worry about what your boring and lazy buddies think. This is for the men who will say, "I'm all in." This isn't for the faint. This isn't for the weak. These action points are not fluffy little suggestions from a useless, watered down denominational quarterly, and neither are they the "39 Steps on How to Get Your Wife in Bed" from a men's magazine. This is about virtue. This is about valor. This is manhood at its finest and these action points of a true "manhood force" can make our marriages and all their designed intent take a gigantic leap toward reality. It's not because some new fact was discovered and written about. Instead, it is because God's original plan was uncovered and lived out.

The day the Spirit of God showed me this picture it completely changed my belief and direction about the concept of being a complete force. It was a gigantic ah-ha moment, and every man I shared it with that day had the same awakening to its power. They all got it. It was THE defining moment.

In the previous chapter I talked about a force moving mountains, clearing paths, changing destinies and having great influence, and I will never back down from that one bit. But there is a force that we already possess, if you know the Father of the Ultimate Force. If it has been covered up for too long, it is time its power and might are awakened and unleashed. When it does it's one that can draw your wife to you stronger than ever or even draw her to you once again. It's the power of being the "Ultimate Magnetic Force."

I was reading a book about business and there was a small two or three page section about the power and force of magnets, how they work, and their attractive capabilities. The very moment I read it God made it all abundantly clear. This force of magnetism draws an object to itself by the power of its molecular makeup, and doesn't only pertain to certain metals. Its power is part of the total package that a Man of Standing possesses. As real men we all want to be the best, create the

But the force of attraction, the force of magnetism is the force and power that draws our precious wives to us with a magnetic field like we've only imagined.

wealth, be the hero, conquer kingdoms, hit the winning shot, slay the dragons…and the list goes on and on. But those types of force are ones that shatter obstacles out of our way with great strength and might. But the force of attraction, the force of magnetism is the force and power that draws our precious wives to us with a magnetic field like we've only imagined.

I love magnets. They're about an 8 out of 10 on my cool-factor scale. I never knew until recently how they worked because I never listened to the lectures in my Chemistry class, which clearly explains my final grade. But as a kid I loved to play with them, and the stronger the magnets the cooler they were. Two pieces of metal that would either come together with such force or be repelled away from each other with the same velocity. At our house they're mostly used to hang the pictures of our kids on the refrigerator door to remind us who's coming over for dinner Sunday night! But if you study what a magnet is and how it works and apply it to this journey of "standing" it can become a life changing experience for your manhood and your marriage.

Since you probably didn't listen in your Chemistry class either, let's take a recap on magnets and magnetic fields. A magnet is an object that produces a thing called a magnetic field, and this field is normally described as a series of lines called, and are you ready for this? Lines of *Force*! And these lines of force run all the way form the north pole of the magnet to the south pole of the magnet. The entire makeup of the magnet has the properties of magnetic force and when the right metal object comes within the range of the magnetic field of that force it is naturally and powerfully drawn to the magnet!

It gets even better. Take two nails that haven't been magnetized and hold them up against each other. Because neither are magnets nothing attracts the one to the other. No force at work. No force, no attraction because neither nail is magnetic. Sound like the current state of your romance? Within the makeup of those nails are millions of atoms that cluster together creating little domains, and those domains are all over the place pointed in all different directions. There is no order. Whereas if you study a magnetic object you'll find it's millions of atoms clustered together creating their own domains are in sequence, in order and lined up pole to pole creating magnetic properties. Now, place the non-magnetic item against the magnet and not only will it attach to it but if you keep the two objects attached for a period of time the dysfunctional, out of aligned atoms of the non-magnetic object begin to come into proper sequence and order, and it too becomes magnetic. Leave it attached to the magnet long enough and even when you take it away from the magnet the atoms stays in order and the object can stay magnetic! This object that can be magnetized or drawn to a magnet is called ferromagnetic and in Physics ferromagnetism is the strongest type of a magnet and is the one that creates a force so strong that it can be felt! Welcome Boaz and Ruth!

Here we had this champion of force with all his magnetism entering into the domain of a beautiful woman who had gone through hell and back only to find herself in the field of *force* of this champion. The closer he approached her the more powerful the magnetic field became, and when he reached her his force of standing went out from the one to the other and history was made. The missing and misaligned properties in life that were the domain of Ruth connected with the lines of force from domain of Boaz. Sparks ignited. An attraction happened. Passion was reborn. Desires were fulfilled. Two lives from two worlds became one and a new destiny became real.

Now, let's plainly state the obvious. In no way am I saying that men are perfect and women are not, so don't even start down that path, and this is not a book to prove we're the kings and our wives are nothing more than dysfunctional peasant girls in desperate need of our biceps. No, these words are to wake all of us up in order that we might reign as kings in this life so the queens of our lives can too reign in their God given destiny. Bottom line, when we as men are fully living out our role as Men of Standing, then our wives don't have to fulfill her role and ours at the same time. Life becomes the way it was created to be.

Whether he knew it or not. Whether he planned it or not. When Boaz came onto the scene and into her life he did four things that made such an indescribable impact on her that falling in love happened effortlessly. He probably did a lot more than four but these are the ones that were recorded in chapter 2 of Ruth. They worked for him then and they most certainly can work for us today. Look at chapter 2:

> So Boaz said to Ruth, "My daughter, listen to me. Don't go and glean in another field and don't go away from here. Stay here with the women who work for me. Watch the field where the men are harvesting, and follow along after the

women. I have told the men not to lay a hand on you. And whenever you are thirsty, go and get a drink from the water jars the men have filled."

At this, she bowed down with her face to the ground. She asked him, "Why have I found such favor in your eyes that you notice me—a foreigner?"

And then in verse 14-16:

At mealtime Boaz said to her, "Come over here. Have some bread and dip it in the wine vinegar."

When she sat down with the harvesters, he offered her some roasted grain. She ate all she wanted and had some left over. As she got up to glean, Boaz gave orders to his men, "Let her gather among the sheaves and don't reprimand her. Even pull out some stalks for her from the bundles and leave them for her to pick up, and don't rebuke her."

First Boaz pursued her. Look at the verse. So Boaz said to Ruth, "My daughter, listen to me. Don't go and glean in another field and don't go away from here." From the time he first laid eyes on her he knew this was real and he was going to make sure there was no way she was ever going anywhere else. He knew what he wanted, for her to never leave and go find something or someone else. He made it clearly known that he wanted her to stay. And he did it in a way that is the perfect model for us as men today. He verbalized it. He actually communicated. And I'll bet you any amount of money that as he was making his romantic desires known for her his eyes and everything that made up his total being and attention were completely on her. I can promise you he wasn't looking over the field making sure all his employees were in order while he was talking, and I can guarantee you he wasn't checking email, voice mail, or any sports scores on his smart-scroll (smart phones in BC days). He was fixed on her. Laser vision. Nothing else mattered. Nothing else grabbed his attention. Not a camel. Not an employee. Not another woman. Not one stalk of wheat or anything else pertaining to his business. She was the focus and the centerpiece of his thoughts and there was no doubt to anyone standing there if he was serious or not. Simply put, he made the main thing the only thing, and the same needs to be said of you today. Are you actively, daily, romantically, passionately, genuinely, with everything you've got virtuously pursuing your wife? Better asked, do you virtuously pursue her in marriage like you pursued her when the two of you were dating?

When Liz and I were dating I was a flower man. For no reason other than I was madly in love with her I'd send her flowers and some of the people she worked with would just roll their eyes. But she didn't. Her eyes would shine. I was daily pursuing her with everything I had. We went out every night we were dating and engaged and unless her mother fixed dinner we were at a restaurant and it wasn't a hot dog stand either, it was steak! Not to win her love, because we knew on our first date we were getting married. I did it because it was the most natural thing for me to do. It didn't have to be a holiday or a special occasion. It was just done on any day, everyday. In the words of the country music group Rascal Flatts, "I love to love you out loud!" And I did.

How's it going with your pursuit? When was the last time your wife, without question, knew you were pursuing her as a person and not just for her body? That friendship and relationship take far more precedence than sex and a hot date. Don't get me wrong. Nothing wrong with being a heat seeking missile, done right with virtue and valor. I love great dates but sometimes you must go back to where you lost your edge, and where the priorities of a virtuous pursuit were lost and led to the issues of the mediocre marriage.

Go back to your first dates. Go back to the night you proposed. Surprise her and show her you want her to fall in love with you again and this time to the deepest level possible. Go back and take a look at the model of pursuit that Boaz did for his future bride. But more than anything else go look and study the greatest love manual ever written and see how the Son of God with all His radiant perfection pursued His bride, the church, like no other bride has ever been pursued before. And you'll find out He loves her with a kind of love that caused Him to lay down His life for her so she could be without a spot or a wrinkle or a blemish. True, virtuous pursuit has become a lost art but it's something a man of standing longs to do and something his wife loves to receive.

The second magnetic action that flowed out of Boaz was to let her know that she was under his protection and nothing was ever going to hurt her much less even touch her. Look at verse 9, "Watch the field where the men are harvesting, and follow along after the women. *I have told the men not to lay a hand on you.*"

As men we don't need any explanation for that statement. We're all guys. We all know what Boaz just said and how he meant it. Bank on it. Boaz, at some point before this conversation took his horse and with a man's man authority, quickly road around and looked at every single one of his men eye to eye, and probably every man within 100 yards, and let it be clearly known if anyone was stupid enough to even think of taking advantage of this young lady, or even had the thought of anything less than treating her like a queen, they would quickly feel his wrath. He might have been a little older than most of those guys he would have to face should one of them think he could take on the boss, but rest assured had there be a fight that young field worker would have had his butt kicked till his nose bled.

Now, let's put this into everyday prospective for our own wives. There's a lot more to this thing called protection than just the physical side. One of the greatest intrinsic needs of a woman is security. Physical security is important, but just as important are the emotional, financial, spiritual, and any other area that's a priority to her. If it's a priority to her then it should be a priority to you. If you want to see mounting pressure build and take a toll on your wife, then relinquish or neglect any one of these and let it spin out of control. Watch and see how the mood changes in your home.

Now, in any marriage there are going to be seasons where for one reason or another there will be some hardship and some uncertain, troubling times. Sometimes it might come from so many directions at once that even Superman would struggle and stumble under the strain. And try as hard as you might, you still crumble under the weight of the pressure. It's at times like these that as men we need to run to our Daddy and I don't mean our earthly one. I'm talking about Abba, our Heavenly Daddy who is longing and yearning to hold you, His son, in His arms and show you His complete love that can heal, rescue, and deliver you from all your troubles. King David did it. So did Moses, Jehosophat, Abraham, and many more. There are 66 books within the Bible that are filled with true stories of God's love, His rescuing and redemption. Some of the greatest champions and world changers who ever walked the face of the earth had their moments where things looked more than a little bleak. They were facing absolute annihilation. But as Men of Standing, they each knew who their refuge was and His name was Jehovah. It still is today. He hasn't changed one bit and believe it or not He's waiting on you to come to Him, just like all these great champions of faith did, so He can show you His love and bring you out of the valley and back to where you're destined to be. The amazing thing is that He wants to do this. It is His will to give us the desires of our heart because He is always working for our good and His glory, if your one of His own.

This security thing is huge. As Men of Standing, the need for it must be one of the top priorities of our mission. There are many things that cause our wives to be anxious or have fearful moments. From everyday concerns to the deeply rooted anxieties. I'm not going to take the time to discuss how we can help our wives overcome the fear of things like mice, snakes, spiders, public speaking, and losing family photos. Not demeaning them, I'm just saying that in the big scheme of things these are small in comparison to critical issues like, "Will I be taken care of?" "Will we have enough money to survive?" "Will I be rejected and unloved?" "Will I not be heard?" or "Will I ever be a priority?"

Now, it's gut check time. Stop your reading and seriously consider the genuine concerns of your wife that were just stated. Think about each one. Do not gloss over this as some token exercise you can say you did. Pour over them. Pray over them. For some of you it's going to be the first time you've taken the time to really drill down and know where you're wife is with each of these. No way am I ever going to attempt to speak for their entire gender but I'm confident that most will at some point in their marriage own the apprehension and anxiety of one or more of these concerns.

Security shaken to the core. It's ugly. Hers and ours! And it's excruciatingly painful. Eve felt it. Sarah certainly got a huge taste of it. All wives have at one time or another been hit by that ferocious pain. Some more than others. Whether it's a few times in life that they experience it or even just one time that this evil pressure invades our homes, it is one time too many.

This is a tough one because the hurt that can come with it can be emotionally devastating. But there is hope. There is a way out, Man of Standing. This is where close communion with God is not only vital but it's the only true path that's going to drive you back to the solid ground where you both want to be. I don't mean a shallow, religious, ritualistic half hearted pass at God. I'm talking about the kind relationship with Him that causes real change. Lasting change. A God anointed relationship where His love completely over takes you, your family, and your circumstances. Ephesians 3:19 in the Amplified Bible says:

> [That you may really come] to know [practically, through experience for yourselves] the love of Christ, which far surpasses mere knowledge [without experience]; that you may be filled [through all your being] unto all the fullness of God [may have the richest measure of the divine Presence, and become a body wholly filled and flooded with God Himself]!

Chew on that verse for a while! He is our hope. He is our way out.

I think of David long after Samuel had anointed him King, yet he was running for his life, hiding in caves, probably feeling like he was a million miles away from his intended destiny. It's as if one moment he is praising God for His goodness and then next he seems to be in the pit of despair. We have all been there at one time or another. The amazing thing to me is that David was a worshipper. He praised God Almighty, His Heavenly Father because he knew that at any moment his circumstances could change…and they ultimately did. During those times of hardships and trials David was a worshipper and the same must be stated of you and me. Any one can lift their hands and be glad when the harvest is happening, but it takes a real Man of Standing who knows to stay on his knees and sometimes on his face in praise and worship to the One who like He did for King David will bring you and I out of the caves of hiding and onto the mountain tops of praising.

It is the spiritual responsibility of every woman to make the Lord her security too and not in someone or something else. But let's get this straight. Life at home can be much smoother and much more peaceful when you build strong security in your home, and the greatest way you can bring it is for you to make the Lord your security and ask Him to come in and take control of everything you have.

This is where seeking Him and His love more than ever before can change the way you think and change the way you live. This is where asking yourself those tough questions we all like to avoid are asked, "Has her security even been on my radar screen?" or "Am I all in to bring God's security to my home?" This is where serious soul searching must take place. This is where the line is drawn, the stake is

This is where the line is drawn, the stake is nailed down deep and the decision to no longer cower to the enemy but to live as a mighty warrior is made.

nailed down deep and the decision to no longer cower to the enemy but to live as a mighty warrior is made. This is where you show your wife that you are committed and sold out to the call of protection for her life. The greatest way to show her is to know the only One, the One true God and His Son who will show up as our Shepherd, who makes us not be in lack for any good thing. Who causes us to lie down in green pastures not in dry and parched wastelands. Who leads us beside still waters, not raging seas. Who leads us along paths of righteousness for His Name's sake, not rocky, dangerous terrains just for the heck of it. Who never leads us in but can always lead us out of the valley of the shadow of death. Who makes a table for us in the presence of our enemies where they're actually our footstools. Who crowns us with a crown of love and compassion and not of thorns. His Son already wore that. Who anoints our head with oil and not with trouble. And who causes love and mercy, not trouble and anguish to follow us all the days of our lives. And we get to dwell in His house forever.

Bottom line. As magnetic forces, one of your top goals is to always make sure your wife is not only protected, but at the same time feels protected. If right now you find yourself in the valley of the shadow of death, know that your Heavenly Father didn't lead you there but He can certainly lead you out and keep you from falling onto that path again.

Ruth knew that in Boaz she had it and she made it known in front of everyone present that he was the Man! How is it with you? How bad do you want it? The confidence of protection is one of the greatest keys to a stress less life…for everyone. And it's one of the greatest keys to an incredible marriage. You must learn this one well.

Third, Boaz became a provider. Look at the second part of verse 9. "And whenever you are thirsty, go and get a drink from the water jars the men have filled." He was saying to her, my love, whenever you are thirsty, go and drink all you want from the jars my servants have filled for you. Look at all that happened in that one statement.

He first said, "whenever." I love that word. Whenever! And I love how Boaz meant it when he said it. Whenever! Whenever there is a thirst in your life! I don't care if it's every 30 minutes or it's every 30 seconds! Whenever you're thirsty, go get your desires met from my abundant supply. Do you think it mattered to Boaz how much she drank or how many times she returned to the jars to quench her thirst? Absolutely not! As a matter of fact I'm convinced Boaz would peek over his shoulder ever so often to make sure her thirst was being satisfied from *his* jars, and each time he saw her take a drink he must have been filled to overflowing with a sense of excitement knowing he was the man who was meeting her needs. His sense of manhood was beaming and his testosterone was flowing. He was providing! He was living out one of the chief roles of manhood! And it was for the love of his life!

Then he said for Ruth to drink for the jars "My servants have filled". In other words, "You're not walking down to the river to fetch your own water. No, no…I've got hired help to do that FOR you. You don't work one ounce for it. You just receive it and you just drink it. You just refresh yourself. You just enjoy! Sum it all up and this is what he was saying: "Whenever, receive."

Whenever, receive! Not once a day and work for it. No, it was some of the most romantic yet powerful words a man could ever say to his wife…Whenever, receive! Burn this into your soul. Make this a priority in your life. I want these words to challenge all of us.

I'm absolutely convinced that the overwhelming majority of God's people much less those outside His family are stuck in a poverty mindset filled with old, worn out religious ideas. It's a broken down poverty belief that says it can't be that good. But God clearly says it's so and His Son came to give it to us.

Can you imagine the reactions our wives would have if they heard the words and saw the provision of "whenever, receive" on a consistent basis? Whenever you need something go pick it up. Do you desire a new car? Let's go pick one out! Do you long for a family vacation? Let's take that cruise! Do you hunger for quality time away from the kids so we can reconnect in a deeper way? I'll call the travel agent now! Do you need that spiritual leader back in the home leading and guiding our family? I apologize I got off track. I completely assume that role again now! Whenever, receive!

For those who might think this sounds completely materialistic look at what Romans 8:31-32 says, "What, then, shall we say in response to these things? If God is for us, who can be against us? He who did not spare his own Son, but gave him up for us all—how will he not also, along with him, graciously give us all things?" And in 1 Timothy 6:17, "Command those who are rich in this present world not to be arrogant nor to put their hope in wealth, which is so uncertain, but to put their hope in God, who richly provides us with everything (all things) for our enjoyment."

Get this into your head. God is not against His children having things. He said He gives us all things for our enjoyment! Enjoy them, just don't put your trust in them but let Him be the provider! Remember He is limitless!

One of my favorite stories in the entire Bible is found in 2 Kings 4:1-7.

The wife of a man from the company of the prophets cried out to Elisha, "Your servant my husband is dead, and you know that he revered the LORD. But now his creditor is coming to take my two boys as his slaves."

Elisha replied to her, "How can I help you? Tell me, what do you have in your house?"

"Your servant has nothing there at all," she said, "except a small jar of olive oil."

Elisha said, "Go around and ask all your neighbors for empty jars. Don't ask for just a few. Then go inside and shut the door behind you and your sons. Pour oil into all the jars, and as each is filled, put it to one side."

She left him and shut the door behind her and her sons. They brought the jars to her and she kept pouring. When all the jars were full, she said to her son, "Bring me another one."

But he replied, "There is not a jar left." Then the oil stopped flowing.

She went and told the man of God, and he said, "Go, sell the oil and pay your debts. You and your sons can live on what is left."

Here we have an incredible story of a limitless God. A widow was faced with the loss of a spouse and the potential loss of her two sons as payment for incurred debt. She cried out to the man of God for answers and he gave her three instructions. Go ask all your neighbors for empty jars. Do not ask for just a few. Then go in a pour what you have into all the jars. At this point you're thinking, "Hold on…she only has a little in one jar. How is she going to pour a little into so many?" It's called faith. Without it we can't move mountains, see miracles, be Men of Standing, or live a life full of God's abundance.

So she acts on her faith and goes and follows the instructions given to her. We don't know how many jars she collected but we know it was more than one! Miraculously, as she began to pour, the oil didn't stop flowing. Setting one jar aside she would call out for another and then another. When they ran out of vessels to fill, the oil stopped flowing. She goes back to the prophet and he gives her the final instructions. Go sell the oil, pay off your debts and you and your sons live the rest of your lives on what is left over!

Answer a couple of questions. First, do you think her actions would have been different as to the number of vessels she borrowed if she knew on the front end what she discovered on the back end? Of course they would have. Do you think she might have wanted a do-over? Without question, if she knew they'd all be filled she would have collected so many vessels you

> *First, do you think her actions would have been different as to the number of vessels she borrowed if she knew on the front end what she discovered on the back end?*

wouldn't have been able to step foot in her house! Second, do you think it would it have mattered if she collected 20 vessels, 20,000 vessels or 20 million vessels? Absolutely not, because the God of the universe knows no limits and He hasn't changed one bit. The King of the universe is trying to teach us that with the capacity you believe in Him, will be the capacity you will receive. All she had was "just a little oil." Her instructions, "Don't just ask for a few" and when the capacity was used up the oil stopped flowing. When Peter is catching fish in Luke 5, the fish filled all the nets and both boats began to sink. Then it stopped when the vehicle was at capacity. Don't ever predetermine or set any limits on the flow and the blessing of God. Never limit Him in anything. We must have an unlimited capacity to receive. It flows until we stop it with our human limitations, our business models, bank accounts and our minds. Ephesians 3:20 states that He can do exceedingly, abundantly more than we can ask or think. Find an unlimited dream for your marriage and your family and with an unlimited mind and faith in God Almighty ask Him to fill it with His limitless Kingdom. God wants to take His limitless power and pour it into your lives, and do things for you that causes your neighbors and the world to stop and take notice.

So who puts the limits on God and His blessings and provision on our lives? We do because of a lack of knowledge and unbelief. Don't let the enemy of your marriage and your home deceive you another minute about God's strong desire to provide us all things.

Are you telling me that when we live up to our full covenant potential as Men of Standing that there isn't going to be a lack in the checkbook? Just how big is our God? How limitless is He? We've limited God by our own limited thinking and limited words we have spoken over ourselves, our marriages, our homes and our destinies. God is bigger than it all. Be bold in your prayers. Be courageous in your petitions. Jabez was. So was David. The bible is filled with Men of Standing who knew their covenant right to boldly approach the throne of grace with Boldness knowing that God Almighty Himself says He gives us all things for our enjoyment.

One last thing about providing and again let's get real. In your home and in your life your paycheck may come through your business or work but the true provision comes from God. He is our provider.

Our paycheck is not our source, and the sooner we learn this truth the more the Lord can show you His will and His plans for you. The Word of God promises you that His blessings are greater than anything you can ask for or even imagine. Seeking Him first and allowing Him to be your provider helps place you into His Kingdom and allows Him to be intimately involved in your everyday lives. And just like Ruth, it's nothing we have to work for. It's His grace at work in our lives because of His good pleasure. Two words that can change both our spiritual walk and our marriage. Whenever, receive!

The last of the four things that Boaz did was he pampered her. Look at verse 14:

> At mealtime Boaz said to her, "Come over here. Have some bread and dip it in the wine vinegar." When she sat down with the harvesters, he offered her some roasted grain. She ate all she wanted and had some left over. As she got up to glean, Boaz gave orders to his men, "Let her gather among the sheaves and don't reprimand her. Even pull out some stalks for her from the bundles and leave them for her to pick up, and don't rebuke her."

He pampered her with the owner's food. He poured out to her the best he had and he gave her all that she needed, all that she wanted, and she had some left over! Then, unknown to her, he played a little trick and told the men to intentionally lay out more stalks of grain for her to pick up as he continued to supply her need and build her self esteem. He refused to allow even a single negative word be said to her. He was doing everything he could at this point in their new relationship to make her life as easy as possible. That's called pampering.

Today it looks a lot different but has the exact same intention. You know what pampering is. It's treating your wife like a queen. It's the backrub or the foot rub even when you're tired and expect nothing in return. It's the coupons for the massage. It's the bubble bath without the kids around. It's the unexpected card or love note. It's the consistent words of praise and encouragement. It's the complete devotion, total faithfulness and undivided attention just to name a few. It's being her Man of Standing!

Pamper, provide, protect, and pursue. Put them in any order. Wrap them up any way you want to. They all spell love. That's it! He just loved her. Her past meant nothing. Her present circumstances meant nothing. There was nothing Boaz was holding against Ruth. All her mistakes. All her past. Whatever she'd done or been through didn't amount to a blip on his radar screen. Even her upbringing and her family heritage flew in one ear and completely out the other. He simply loved her. Believe it or not that's just like my Abba with me today, and you too if you have received His Son. He doesn't care about our past. He's not holding it against us and He's certainly trying to get us out of any and every ditch that we may fall into. Why? Because He perfectly loves us and has granted to all His children His unmerited favor called grace. Remember He said in Romans 5:17 that He has freely given us His abundance of His unmerited favor, His grace. Unmerited, not based on one single type of performance on my part. That's why it's called UN-merited favor. And He's bestowed on all His children His gift of righteousness. The very act of being in right standing with the Father…right now, once again free from any of our performance. That's the love of my God. That was the love of Boaz. And men, let's get extremely real. That should be the love we have for our spouse right now.

I know what many of you are thinking. "Yeah Jim, that's sounds real spiritual but you don't live with my wife, and you don't know all the hell she puts me trough on a daily basis." You're right. I don't and I don't pretend to be a marriage counselor either. She might be putting you through what seems like hell so why don't you allow her to see heaven in you. Love her even though according to our worldly, fleshy way of thinking she doesn't deserve it. Just love her anyway. Just love her. When she treats you like crap, love her. When she's in a bad mood, love her. When she's in pain and hurt from a disconnected dad that causes such agony and more questions than answers in her life, and you seem to be the target, just love her. When she's lost in her own world, just love her; and when you're not a priority in that world just… you guessed it, love her.

By the way, the Word says "that while we were sinners, Christ died for us." Did you get that? The Lord of the universe went on a death mission to seek and to save all who were lost. To those who would receive Him but just as much for those who would never believe Him or ever call on His name. Those who could have cared less about Him or anything He stood for. The vile, the ugly, the perverted, the spiritually mangled devastated wrecks were His mission to bring into a love relationship with Him and not only breathe into them life but to give them the perrisos life…remember?

He is our model. He left for us the perfect blueprint for success. That's our mission. Are you man enough for it?

CHAPTER 7

SLINGING STONES
AND SLAYING GIANTS

Nothing had worked. Every single one of them was terrified. Literally shaking in their boots where they stood. For 40 long days their manhood had been challenged. For 40 embarrassing days they had been laughed at, taunted, told they were cowards and would soon be thrown into slavery forever. They were being emotionally and mentally tortured, day by day, moment by moment. How could this happen? They were trained soldiers. The best of the best. They thought they had seen it all, but never had they seen an enemy soldier who stood over 9 feet tall. Fully armed with a spear that most men couldn't maneuver much less use as a weapon because of its weight. And there he stood. For over a month he had come out every day, arrogantly pointing his ugly pagan finger at the Israelite army laughing at them knowing that soon they would

94

engage in the battle and lose or surrender all together. That is, until the day the hero showed up.

Word quickly spread throughout the troops that someone had come who would fight to defend their honor and defeat this giant. Someone was putting on the armor and was preparing for battle. Someone was about to set them free from their suffering of humiliation and fears. There's movement and commotion at the back of the lines. The warrior is trying to get through so he can destroy this enemy of God's people. The soldiers on the front lines felt a sense of courage they had not experienced in almost a month and a half. The front line separates so all can see this mighty champion, especially this giant. He's got to be huge! He must be a stud! And out walks…a boy. And if that's not bad enough, a shepherd boy!

Talk about laughter. The Philistine army, led by their giant laughed so hard that I bet he had to bend over and put his hands on his knees just to keep from falling to the ground. A place he'd soon find himself! It was hilarious to the Philistines. It was humiliating to the Israelites. No armor? No sword? No man-made protection? And what does he have in his hand, a sling? Every Philistine was laughing. Every Israelite was crying. Except for one. The only one who counted and his name was David! The anointed king of Israel. Without a shred of doubt, with absolute confidence in his God and being fully persuaded about the outcome, this shepherd boy looks this pagan giant over from head to toe and with a Clint Eastwood squint in his eyes and a Rocky Balboa "go for it" tone in

The Philistine army, led by their giant laughed so hard that I bet he had to bend over and put his hands on his knees just to keep from falling to the ground. A place he'd soon find himself!

his voice, and he tells this soon to be headless hit man what's he's about to do to him.

"You come against me with a sword and spear and javelin, but I come against you in the name of The Lord Almighty, the God of the armies of Israel, whom you have defiled. This day the Lord will deliver you into my hands and I'll strike you down and cut off your head. This very day I will give the carcasses of the Philistine army to the birds and the wild animals, and the whole world will know there is a God in the house of Israel. All those gathered here will know that it is not by sword or spear that the Lord saves; for the battle is the Lord's and He will give all of you into our hands."

As the Philistine moved closer to attack him. David ran quickly toward the battle line to meet him. Reaching into his bag and taking out a stone he slung it and struck the Philistine on the forehead. The stone sank into his forehead and he fell facedown on the ground.

So David triumphed over the Philistine with a sling and a stone; without a sword in his hand he struck down the Philistine and killed him.

David ran and stood over him. He took hold of the Philistine's sword and drew it from his sheath. After he killed him, he cut off his head with the sword.

When the Philistines saw that their hero was dead, they turned and ran. Then the men of Israel and Judah surged forward with a shout and pursued the Philistines to the entrance of Gath and the gates of Ekron. Their dead were strewn along the Shaaraim road to Gath and Ekron. When the Israelites returned from chasing the Philistines, they plundered their camp.

David took the Philistines head and brought it to Jerusalem: he put the Philistines weapon in his own tent! (1 Samuel 17:45-54)

I swear, I had so much adrenaline flowing in me after just reading that story and putting it on paper I had to stop and go lift some weights! It just explodes with testosterone. Go back and read the full account. David stares down this almost 10 foot tall mountain of a man in the eyes and tells him exactly what he's going to do to him, and this is right after Goliath tried to scare David by telling him what turns out he only thought he was going to do. This is the turning point of the story. Goliath roars out what he thinks is about to happen and David mocks him openly. Shaming him in front of both armies by telling him not only are you not going to do that to me but now since you said it, that's exactly what I'm going to do to you, you punk!

I love 1 Samuel Chapter 17. It's true a story everyone has heard, but when you move away from this just being a great motivational story to being totally convinced this really happened, it becomes a model for us as men. This epic event captures what true valor, courage, and bravery looks like, and clearly models for all of us what it should look like today in our lives and in our homes.

It's a story of unshakable faith. Think about the faith David possessed to be able to stand up against the giant. Think about the faith David had to possess to stand up against the disbelief of his own brothers. It's this same level of "God confidence" you must possess if you want to destroy the giants that are raging wars of fear and doubt in your marriages and families. We all want to slay the giant but are we courageous enough to engage in the fight?

David wasn't scared. Nothing in scripture even remotely hints of him being nervous. This warrior didn't show any sign of panic. He didn't quietly backtrack his steps or his words. Instead he kept asking the soldiers what he'd get if he took down Goliath. He even said to those on the front line, "Who is this uncircumcised Philistine that he should defy the armies of the living God!" No waiver of unbelief. No double mindedness. He didn't even pay his enemy the respect of calling him by his name. To David he was nothing more than "the uncircumcised Philistine!" David powerfully carried a complete confidence in God Almighty into the battle because he recognized that Goliath and everything he stood for was not in covenant relationship with God like he was. Goliath was the enemy! People in a covenant relationship with God have all the blessings of God in them and all the backing of heaven around them. Even though Goliath looked more powerful than any Israelite soldier, David was the only one who knew Goliath truly had no power over him or any other Israelite warrior, except the power they handed over to him. David understood his covenant relationship with God, and so must you discover for yourselves that nothing outside the covenant promises you have been given as children of God should be ruling over your lives and your homes.

You'll find the kind of faith that David carried with him all throughout the Bible. Champions who refused to back down. Warriors who didn't look to the right or the left but firmly guarded their heart and kept their eyes solely on God, and refused to wavier in their belief even during unspeakable odds. David also didn't listen to the people in the crowd who were staggering with unbelief. These soldiers knew they were God's chosen people and they knew they were supposed to be reigning in life, but for those forty days life had been raining on them. There was about to be a war on the outward battlefield before them, but they were already engaged in an even larger conflict that was taking place on the battlefield within them.

Fear is a horrible thing to be controlled by. Its grip can be so powerful it sometimes doesn't even allow you to make simple, sound decisions. Look at the situation in this story. They were so controlled by fear they didn't even try to use tactical, strategic military moves to kill Goliath. What about someone sneaking into camp in the middle of the night and take him out? Poison his food? An unexpected long range bow and arrow shot? Something! And who said that Goliath got to set the rules for the fight? Every day this emotionally paralyzed army let the enemy stack the deck and set the rules for their lives and the enemy continues to do the same thing today. Yet it is during those dark times of confusion and even despair that you must determine in your heart if you're going to live like the soldiers who were emotionally paralyzed with fear, or are you going to live like David who was completely convinced that God not only had the power to do what he said He would do but also have the desire to do it.

Not only was his faith unshakable but his courage was fearless. Here comes this young man whose blood pressure doesn't go up one level as he looks over the situation and sizes up the giant. He doesn't take on the mindset of everyone else who were saying, "He's so big we can't stop him." But David's thought was, "He's so big I can't miss him!"

David spoke out his actions and his destiny to the giant before he ever did them. He literally spoke it into existence. He faced the giant and repeated back to him what he had originally said to David but when David spoke those same words back he added in the "Name of The Lord Almighty, The God of the armies of Israel." Goliath spoke curses. David spoke covenant. David gives the reason for the victory he's about to experience. "So the whole world will know there's a

God in the house of Israel!" There it is. The reason for David's victory then and the reason for your victory today. So the whole world will know there a God in the house of your family. God wants our lives to be full of His victories. His desire is for us to win. He wants us to dominate. Why? So the whole world will know there is a God in the house of your family.

The world never has, and never will listen to dull, boring, lifeless messages or messengers, but it will seek out, promote, and follow those who champion their mission. God Almighty created us. He put His DNA of domination in us so the whole world will know there is a God in the house of Israel.

David also took into battle the talents and strengths that God had given him. He carried the anointing and power of God, and destroyed the giant that conventional soldiers with conventional weapons using a conventional battle plan couldn't do. He wouldn't even carry into battle the suit of armor Saul tried to make him wear. It didn't fit. It wasn't him and it was something he had absolutely no confidence in. He told the king that he had killed the lion and the bear with his hands and this giant was no different than any other wild animal. After it was over and the Israelite army was crowned victors, it was all because of one young man who didn't care what he looked like or how he sounded. David didn't waste one second of his life worrying what anyone thought about him or his ways of doing something. He could have cared less. He was absolutely secure in the power and anointing of God, and he carried that along with his ammo and killed a giant that changed the destiny of his life and the lives countless others. He gave us an incredible story of a "God anointed, out of the box, could care less what anyone thinks about it" account of bravery and he got it done. Right now, ask God to make your heart one of bravery and valor, and to give you confidence as you take up the mission for Him.

Sometimes God uses the most unusual things and people to accomplish His plans. If you want great victories, if you desire to win the prize then prepare to do it God's way. And many times it's not going to look like a conventional battle plan. How do you think David would have done had he gone into battle wearing Saul's armor? He'd got knocked around until he said, "Enough with this junk that's weighing me down, just give me my sling!" When you come to the point where you are fed up with the worlds thinking and reasoning and are willing to listen to the One who has all the right answers, then and only then will lasting victory be yours.

One more thing about this battle story. After it was all said and done I wonder how many soldiers in the Israelite army quietly started practicing with a sling?

I've read this story many times over the last few years and each time I read it and then really listen, God unveils a truth to me to put it into action into my own life and circumstances. There are countless numbers of powerful, destiny changing truths in this chapter. I want to give you seven.

1. David knew who he was. Even though he never said it, he was the anointed King of Israel. God's authority and power had been taken away from Saul and now rested with David. God sent the great prophet Samuel to anoint the next king and He led him straight to David. Even though David had seven older brothers who all looked the part, none fit the bill. After seeing all of David's brothers Samuel even asked David's father if he had any more sons. "There is still the youngest,"

David's father answered, "but he is tending the sheep." (1 Samuel 16:11) God is so awesome! The world would have looked at the older brothers and said, "Eliab, now there's a stud. He's 6'4" and weighs 225 pounds. He can bench press 350 lbs and runs a forty yard dash in 4.4 seconds." And God says, "No, not him." "Well then it must be Abinadad! He's 6'5" and a chiseled 215 lbs." And God says, "Not him either." Not to say David was a scrawny kid because he wasn't. He was rugged and handsome but God was looking at the heart! And He found a man who was "after His own heart." So Samuel anointed David and from that day on David grew in strength and power.

David knew who he was and it defined who he became. The same holds true with you today. Who and what you think you are will ultimately define what you become, so it's incredibly important to discover what the Creator of the universe says about His children. The key phrase here is, His children.

> *David knew who he was and it defined who he became.*

"But you are a chosen people, a royal priesthood, a holy nation, a people belonging to God." (1 Peter 2:9) We are now condemnation free people. (Romans 8:1) We are loved and individually chosen by God Himself (1 Thessalonians 1:4) We are individually crafted and designed by the Creator of the universe and have been given a mission to accomplish (Eph 2:10) We are redeemed, delivered, liberated and forgiven by the riches of His undeserved merit (Ephesians 1:7) We have been made holy and blameless in His sight (Ephesians 1:4) and we have become the righteousness of God in Christ (2 Cor. 5:21) and yes, we have become a child of God (John 1:12) with full rights to heirs as son of God (Romans 8:17).

I will state it again. Who and what you think you are will ultimately define what you become. Doesn't it make sense that you learn who you are from the One who designed and created you? The One who put His seal upon you. The One who drafted out a plan for all of us and not from the worlds perspective or even religious falsehoods! Rise up Man of Standing. This is who you are!

Notice there is no mention of the word sinless, perfect, or a worm in any of His descriptions of us. Sure we sin. No we're not perfect and in no way shape or form are we worms. If you are in Christ then you are sons of The Most High God. Do you always live like it? Absolutely not. But you will begin to the day you receive a new revelation of your true identity. If you listen to how the world defines you then you'll become enamored with yourself and if you listen to how the devil defines you then just like the Israelite soldiers you will be defeated by his lies. Listen only to the One who created you. His plans are for your good.

2. David told the giant what he was going to do to him and he went out and did it. Not only did the giant clearly hear him but so did both armies. From what was within his heart David clearly spoke it out and even though everyone around him was screaming that he was crazy, David refused to back down one inch. He had burned his ships. For David, there was no going back.

No one would have blamed him had he stepped out and surveyed the situation and then quietly stepped back only to get lost in the crowd. Who could say a word? Certainly not the soldiers who daily refused to engage in the battle themselves. After all he was just a shepherd boy with a bag of stones, but knowing who he was and the anointing on his life empowered David to rise up and destroy the enemy of God's people. After all, his nature was that of a shepherd, and the most natural thing to do when he saw his sheep become afraid and in danger was to rise up and kill the enemy. He loved his sheep and he wanted no harm to come to them and so in his eyes this giant was nothing more to him than a lion or a bear. And if God empowered him with strength and bravery to kill two of the fiercest animals, then why would his Heavenly Father, the perfect Shepherd, change in mid stream and not let him once again deliver the sheep from destruction?

David listened long enough to the giant as he babbled his toothless threats. I don't even think he let the Philistine finish all that he wanted to say, but David had heard enough, and he proceeded to let Goliath know his very imminent future and then he did it. He kept his word. He did what he said he was going to do, and here is the lesson as men we must learn. If you want to kill the giants that stand in the way of you having the marriage of your dreams, then one of the greatest things you must do is honor your words and do what you say you will do, regardless of the odds. It started on the wedding day with the vows you made, and it continues everyday for the rest of your life.

You promised to love, honor, cherish, and protect her forever. As the human shepherd of your home you are responsible for the tending and the raising of your family. If you're watching, if you're truly attentive to the condition of your home you'll not only be able to detect a giant sent to destroy, but you'll take it down with the power of the Word of God.

One of my earthly hero's is my dad. Unlike many children today my family was blessed to have a man whose mission in life was to be everything he could be for his wife and two children. My mom and dad had been married for over 51 years when my mom was diagnosed with a disease that shortly thereafter took her life. The last four days of her life were spent at home in a coma under the care of hospice. My mom was a champion. She rose every morning at 4:30 a.m. to pray for her family. She and dad had spent the last 16 years of their lives together tutoring children to read and work math problems. She taught phonics even though she was deaf in one ear, but being totally convinced this was her mission she loved on those kids. They had prayer everyday in their homemade classrooms and sometimes they would teach up to 30 students a day out of their house from 6:00 a.m. until 6:00 p.m. or later.

Those last four days of her life here on earth we watched as over 100 people came to pray over her and say their goodbyes. Many of those same kids she had served were now grown with their own kids who came and spoke a blessing over her emaciated body. A couple of nights before she passed I was sitting in the kitchen around midnight with my dad. He was exhausted. His best friend was leaving him and he had been constantly at her side for 51 years, always loving, always providing, and always being a real man to her. We were sitting at the bar in the kitchen where as a family we had eaten thousands of meals over the years, and I looked at him and told him how proud I was of him and then I told him that he was my hero. Without pause my dad just looked at me and said, "I'm just doing what I said I would do 51 years ago." I was speechless. This man who was always there for his family just laid out for his son words that every man needs to hear. "I'm just doing what I said would do."

It's time to revisit your wedding vows men. It's time to rethink your priorities. From the small things that might seem meaningless to us but huge to her, all the way to most important things that are critical for the success of your home. It's time you learn that one of the greatest things as men you can do is honor your commitments and keep your word. All those soldiers who were there that day heard what David said and then witnessed what David did and there was no difference between the two. David kept his word to Goliath! Men of Standing keep their word to their families.

3. The Bible said that as the giant moved closer to attack, David ran to the battle line to meet him. Notice the difference. The giant moves closer. David is running. It's as if there are two different mindsets causing there to be two different speeds. Goliath knows there's something different about this opponent. After all, for 40 days Goliath has watched as trained soldiers shook in their boots as he laughed and mocked them openly. But this kid was different. There was no shaking in his steps. No cracking in his voice and not one drop of nervous sweat running down his brow. He saw that David was locked in on him so he simply approached, but David was in a dead run to get there. David was fearless. He was unafraid. He was mad and he had the giant in his crosshairs! "How dare you defy the army of the Living God?" And before the uncircumcised Philistine knew what hit him he was dead. David might have played the harp in the band and might have baby-sat sheep in the pasture, but that day

as he stood over his victim and defeated the enemy he was a warrior. That day King David came onto the scene. Rise up men, your destiny is waiting on you.

Here are two scriptures to emblazon into your life. Don't just read them. Don't just memorize them. Second graders can do that. Powerless preachers do that every Sunday. No, put them down into the very core of your spirit. Allow them to become who you are.

First, in Isaiah 60:1. The Word says "Arise and Shine." The word Arise in the Hebrew is the word Quwm and it means "to rise", "stand up", to arise and become powerful", "to be established", "to be fixed", "to arise and come onto the scene". If you read Isaiah 60 you'll find there are many promises that God has promised for those who follow His word. Wealth, honor, peace, victory wherever you go. Peace in your home! Your business bringing you the wealth of nations 24 hours a day but the number one contingent command is to arise. Come onto the scene in a militant way.

Second, in 2 Peter 1:4, Peter tells us that as sons of God we now can become partners of the divine nature and escape the corruption of the world caused by evil desires. The word "become" in the Greek is the word ginomai and it means "to become", "to come into existence", "begin to be", "appear in history", "come upon the stage". God is imploring His children to rise up and come on the scene. To rise up and appear in history. To rise up and come onto the stage. The world is waiting for you to appear. It's begging and groaning for you to appear, but like the Israelite soldiers you've been hiding in the crowd far too long. God Almighty is commanding His sons and daughters to rise up make a difference! All of creation is groaning for the Sons of God to reveal themselves and it's time you do. Stop

Find out who you are, what you're supposed to do, and then with courageous faith given to you by God Himself run to the front line. Your victory is waiting on you there.

being passively lost in the crowd. Success will never be found there. Neither will the desires of your heart. Find out who you are, what you're supposed to do, and then with courageous faith given to you by God Himself run to the front line. Your victory is waiting on you there.

4. David discovered who he was and matured in that discovery while he was all alone on a hillside tending his sheep. When Samuel anointed David the new King he didn't go out and sign a contract with an agent. No speaking tour. No book deal. No jerseys being sold with David's name and number on it. He received the anointing and went back to the hillside with his harp and tended the sheep. I am convinced it was in those solitary hours of worship that his identity, his faith, and his destiny were forged in his heart. So it must be with us. Great victories happen outwardly in your homes because of the solitude time you spend on your own mountain in worship. This is not child's play. This is not your typical "quiet time." This is not your basic, "Now I lay me down to sleep," prayer. This is serious stuff. This is where kingdoms collide. This is where the supernatural is brought forth into the natural. This is where miracles occur and this is where many times the battle is won.

This is time on your knees. This is time on your face. This is time with your hands in the air praying, petitioning, praising and worshipping the One who owns it all. This is where your destiny is forged and this is where you see the hand of God move.

Babies aren't born overnight. There's growth that must take place within the womb that no one can see. Gold medals aren't placed around the necks of those who showed up at the gym just every once in a while, and giants aren't slain by those who are half-hearted and too busy to get in the game.

David didn't have to think about what to do or even draw up a battle plan. His Kingship warrior traits kicked in and I believe that happened because he was ready. He was ready because of those one-on-one times with God. So it must be with you as you too find those solitary times and places where you discover your true nature. Where God's truth is revealed and our eyes and hearts are opened to our loving Father, and His indescribable and unimaginable love is revealed to us. It's finding that love that will shape our lives and bring out our destinies.

5. David refused to let Goliath set the rules. For 40 days the Israelite army had allowed him to do so. For 40 days they would line up for battle hoping that this day would be different, and for 40 days Goliath came out and said the same thing which caused the same reaction from the Israelites…fear. They went to bed and the last thing on their mind was fear. They woke up each morning only to have that same emotion paralyze their thoughts and actions. It became routine with no end in sight. That is until David showed up. It quickly became apparent that Goliath was no longer in charge. He had been the order giver, but when David came onto the scene he changed everything. He took back all the

authority that his fellow Israelites had handed over to the giant and didn't allow it to go on another second! Goliath tried to morally defeat David like he had done to the other soldiers, but David knowing who he was and knowing his mission abruptly put an end to all the threats. Then David set the rules. "You come against me with what you have, but I come against you with what I have and His name is the Lord God Almighty and now here are my rules." "You can walk as slowly or as cautiously as you want to the battle lines but I'll be there waiting on you." And he was. David refused to let the enemy continue to set the rules for his family and neither should you. The same authority that David carried into battle is the exact same God with the exact same authority that you have. Even though there aren't any literal 9 foot tall giants walking around your neighborhood today doesn't mean there aren't other giants that try and rule over your house. Far too many homes have already become enslaved to the world's system that is so subtle yet destructive. If anyone dares to be different they're automatically tagged as weird or out of touch with reality. If you want your kids to be successful and if you want your marriage to be successful, you can't go along with that worldly pressure. Ignore the crowd and stand up for your family. Take back authority where it's been handed over. David did it and it changed his destiny and so can you.

6. The entire Israelite army discovered that all it took was one God anointed man to defeat what was blocking them from victory. When this one giant was defeated it was a massive shot of confidence given to each soldier. What had looked impossible for so long had immediately been destroyed, and

that's all they needed to regain their courage and rout the foreign army.

"When the Philistines saw that their hero was dead, they turned and ran. Then the men of Israel and Judah surged forward with a shout and pursued the Philistines to the entrance of Gath and the gates of Ekron. Their dead were strewn along the Shaaraim road to Gath and Ekron. When the Israelites returned from chasing the Philistines, they plundered their camp."

All it took for the Israelites to find their courage and do what they were trained to do was for the one thing that was blocking them to be defeated. In this instance it was Goliath. What is it with you?

Throughout history destinies were changed because a hero faced an insurmountable Goliath, stared it down and said no longer will you have power over me.

Throughout modern track and field history running faster than a four minute mile was determined to be physically impossible. Our bodies just weren't made for it. Our lung capacity couldn't handle it. No one was ever going to accomplish it. That is until a medical student by the name of Roger Bannister took up the challenge. After a humiliating defeat in a race, he was determined to defy all odds, and become the man who would break the 4 minutes mile. And on May 6th at Iffley track in Oxford England, he did just that. What was once thought to be impossible became doable, and now over the years has become an easy mark for world athletes to blow through. But it took one man who had the determination to look that giant in the eye and say, "No more."

It happened again in Mobile Alabama on December 1, 1955 when a 42 year old African American woman named Rosa Parks was fed up with the giant of racism and refused to move to the back of a bus she was riding on. She faced her giant and told him that he would no longer set the rules. In her autobiography she said, "People always say that I didn't give up my seat because I was tired, but that isn't true. I was not tired physically, or no more tired than I usually was at the end of a working day. I was not old, although some people have an image of me as being old then. I was forty-two. No, the only tired I was, was tired of giving in."

And on a Roman cross over 2000 years ago the greatest giant of all was defeated and crushed when the sinless, spotless, perfect Man of Standing, Jesus the Christ, the Son of the Living God said not "my will" but "thy will" be done, and he faced the giant of sin, wrath, condemnation, sickness, poverty, lack, guilt, and shame and defeated the greatest enemy of us all so that we could now become sons of God with full rights of Sonship!

How many families could be revolutionized if there was a model for men to follow? How many men hiding in the crowd would gain strength and courage to defeat their own Goliaths if there was just one man who said, "I'll be that leader." How many generations could we inspire if our children and grandchildren watched as their fathers and grandfathers rose up to be Men of Standing? It takes just one person, the one the world was crying out to see. History is made, and destinies are changed. Listen to your call.

7. David knew that the battle was not his, but The Lords. The last one, and so important. David says:

"You come against me with a sword and spear and javelin, but I come against you in the name of The Lord Almighty, the God of the armies of Israel, whom you have defiled. This day the Lord will deliver you into my hands and I'll strike you down and cut off your head. This very day I will give the carcasses of the Philistine army to the birds and the wild animals, and the whole world will know there is a God in the house of Israel. All those gathered here will know that it is not by sword or spear that the Lord saves; for the battle is the Lord's and He will give all of you into our hands."

This was God's battle. Yes there was a stone slung and there were swords drawn, but this was God's battle and He delivered all the Philistine army into the hands of the Israelites before any action took place. I don't know where you are today in your battle for your family, but I do know that your battles are God's battles, and He is calling His children to invite Him in and let Him fight on your behalf.

This battle wasn't won because David was tougher than Goliath. He was not. It wasn't won because David had more testosterone than Goliath. It was won because of David's faith in God, period. This battle was won before David even "came onto the scene." It was conceived because of the anointing. It was strengthened on a lonely hillside of worship and it was proven by killing the lion and the bear. This confidence in God carried David throughout his life. David did take one piece of armor with him into battle, the shield of faith!

One anointed man who led his army back to victory and inspired all those watching to get off the sideline and get back in the battle. One stone. One man. One shot heard around the world. Be that man. Keep aggressively speaking the truth. Keep boldly living out your God given dreams and like David, one day a king will call upon you to lead!

David, the slayer of Goliath.

David, protector of his flock.

David, the worshiper on the hillside.

David, the anointed one of Samuel.

David, the great grandson of Boaz!

CHAPTER 8

The Battle in the Night... There Will Always Be One

Gettysburg, Normandy, Midway, the Battle of the Bulge, and the Battle at Trenton. Names and places of some of the most important battles fought and won by American forces that kept our freedoms safe. Yet with each bloody confrontation there were soldiers lost. Countless numbers of soldiers lost from these brutal and atrocious battles and untold more injured, including James Earnest Barrett, my grandfather, who fought in the Battle of the Bulge and brought home a Purple Heart from the war and a new heart from a Spiritual conversion from inside a foxhole.

From the beginning of time wars have been fought over land, oil, gold or for the desire of world domination. But there was a battle fought around 1000 BC that wasn't over any of those things. It was fought for families. It was fought to retake the families of 600 men who had been captured by the enemy and at the center of it all was King David, the mightiest warrior of them all.

David was off busy with life and when his back was turned and his attention distracted, the enemy came in to do what he specializes in…to try to steal, kill, and destroy. This battle is epic. It's heroic and it's without question a model for us as Men of Standing that one day you will have to fight.

We are in war men. Manhood is being attacked today more than ever and we cannot afford to be passive and just hope everything "works itself out" any longer. But, it's not from an army that you can see. We are fighting against the spiritual principalities and powers whose mission is to lure us and our families to destruction and death. If you are going to rescue and deliver yourselves and your families, then you must have a serious awakening to the fact there is a battle going on lead by the same forces that have forever been bent on wiping out the home. If you are going to wage war and defend your family's borders then it will be won by weapons of faith. Not with weapons of this world, but with the spiritual weapons that tear down strongholds. This is our call men. Men of Standing are those who sense the oncoming damage and do whatever needs to be done to rescue those being led to slaughter.

> *We are in war men. Manhood is being attacked today more than ever and we cannot afford to be passive and just hope everything "works itself out"*

The problem is many men don't even know there is a war going on and even worse most men don't want to get involved. "It's too time consuming," or "these kind of things just work themselves out!" And God forbid we'd want to get involved if people start talking about things like spiritual warfare. Most think that stuff is better left alone. "If you don't mess with that stuff it won't mess with you!" "Better to just leave it alone." Wake up. There is a battle going on for your family whether you realize it or not and if you don't then there's going to be some type of spiritual battering ram coming for your own front door.

As men you want your families to be right but do you have the desire to even engage in the battle? This reminds me of a story in Mark 5 where Jesus cast out evil spirits out of a possessed man and into a bunch of pigs. This man had been scaring the entire country side. He was naked. He had ripped the chains off his arms and legs, no one could subdue him, and he would sit in the graveyard and howl and cut himself all day.

Jesus steps in and engages in the war that was taking place inside this man and he was delivered. When the towns people heard what had happened they came out to see him and found him with Jesus. He was sitting down, fully clothed, in his right mind, and at peace. The Bible said the people saw this and became afraid, and they begged Jesus to leave them immediately! Explain that if you can. Here we have a crazed lunatic, naked, spitting, slobbering, breaking chains and howling all night in the graveyard and Jesus fixes the problem, and the same people who a few minutes ago were terrified of this man, are now afraid of Jesus and want Him to go! Why? Here's what the Lord showed me. It was messy! It wasn't conventional. No question they wanted him delivered. They just wanted it their way, something they could explain. Some model that a self-help book could be written about and a formula conceived. But it wasn't any one of those. It was supernatural. It was a battle where authority spoke and those under that authority had to obey. It's the same authority being exercised today that will win the battle for your manhood and for your families.

Around 3000 years ago another evil was about to take place. The enemy brutally ravaged a village taking all the women and children and animals, stealing all the valuables, and burning the rest to the ground.

David had been on the run, hiding from Saul for several years. Saul who had become insanely jealous of David's success and popularity in Israel wanted to kill him, but David kept eluding him. You can read about it in 1 Samuel, chapters 18-26. When you read this section you'll find that when David needed wisdom or revelation for evading Saul, he would seek the Lord and the Lord would always answer him and keep him safe. David walked with God. There were even two occasions where David could have easily killed Saul, but refused because of his Godly honor of the king, even though this ungodly king was trying to kill his son in law David! David would seek the Lord and always escape. At one point during his evasion David is hiding in a cave. He is joined by some of his family and around 400 men who the Bible says were in distress, in debt, and discontented. Sounds like most men today yet, over time, these men were mentored and trained by David. Their number grew to 600 and these became David's mighty men. And with his new army David conquered kingdoms and continued to seek the Lord.

In chapter 27 everything changes. It starts off with:

But David thought to himself, "One of these days I will be destroyed by the hand of Saul. The best thing I can do is to escape to the land of the Philistines. Then Saul will give up searching for me anywhere in Israel, and I will slip out of his hand."

So David and the six hundred men with him left and went over to Achish son of Maok king of Gath. David and his men settled in Gath with Achish. Each man had his family with him, and David had his two wives: Ahinoam of Jezreel and Abigail of Carmel, the widow of Nabal. When Saul was told that David had fled to Gath, he no longer searched for him.

Then David said to Achish, "If I have found favor in your eyes, let a place be assigned to me in one of the country towns, that I may live there. Why should your servant live in the royal city with you?"

So on that day Achish gave him Ziklag, and it has belonged to the kings of Judah ever since. David lived in Philistine territory a year and four months.

So David settles in Ziklag. Maybe he was tired of being hunted. Maybe he was worn out. But it's obvious that a spiritual drift had occurred in his life because instead of doing what he had done for years, seeking the Lord for his protection and guidance, he changed his way of thinking. The Bible said he "thought to himself" and there is a huge difference between the two. David chose his common sense over God's wisdom, and it would cost him. Proverbs 3:5-6 in the Amplified Version says:

"Lean on, trust in, *and* be confident in the Lord with all your heart *and* mind and do not rely on your own insight *or* understanding.

In all your ways know, recognize, *and* acknowledge Him, and He will direct *and* make straight *and* plain your paths.

David, like all of us at one time or another began to rely on his own senses and insight. We live in the world's system 24 hours a day, 365 days a year. Unless we're really, seriously seeking with no other agenda other than to truly know God and His ways, we'll have a very hard time distinguishing between His kingdom and the world's ways of doing things. Going over to the land of the Philistines was a logical and probably a strategic military thing to do. Saul certainly wasn't going to go into enemy territory and risk his life. So Saul gives up hunting David, and now David can rest. But once you move in and settle down in enemy territory, you start to pick up the habits of the people there, which may not always be in line with God. David was no different. He actually finds himself fighting alongside the Philistines against Israel, his own kingdom. This subtle drift had become a slippery slope because now David was about to engage in a deadly battle with the nation God had anointed him to one day lead. In fact right before they went into battle the Philistine leaders recognized David, and actually booted him and his mighty men from their army because they were afraid that David would turn on them in the middle of the battle. David had drifted so far into a dysfunctional funk for whatever reason that now even his enemies refused to let him be a part of their army. The next morning David and all his men left and went back to their families and homes in Ziklag. At least that's what they thought they'd come home to.

1 Samuel 30 says:

David and his men reached Ziklag on the third day. Now the Amalekites had raided the Negev and Ziklag. They had attacked Ziklag and burned it, and had taken captive the women and everyone else in it, both young and old. They killed none of them, but carried them off as they went on their way.

When David and his men reached Ziklag, they found it destroyed by fire and their wives and sons and daughters taken captive. So David and his men wept aloud until they had no strength left to weep. David's two wives had been captured—Ahinoam of Jezreel and Abigail, the widow of Nabal of Carmel. David was greatly distressed because the men were talking of stoning him; each one was bitter in spirit because of his sons and daughters.

The enemy came in and kidnapped the women and children, stole everything they wanted and burned the rest. Their village was destroyed. Their families taken captive. All David and his men were left with was their fear and their imagination of what might be happening to their wives and children at that very moment. These were some of the greatest warriors ever, yet the Bible said they cried aloud until all their strength to cry anymore was gone.

Somewhere in the midst of his excruciating agony David remembered God. He remembered the times he would call out to Him and his deliverance would come. So David, in the midst of unspeakable gMy friend, you have two choices. You can choose to bury your head in the sand hoping it will all go away on its own, or you can choose to do what David

My friend, you have two choices. You can choose to bury your head in the sand hoping it will all go away on its own, or you can choose to do what David did and call upon the Lord and ask Him and His Kingdom to step in to your situation and give you the kind of peace, wisdom, strength and deliverance that can only come from Him.

did and call upon the Lord and ask Him and His Kingdom to step in to your situation and give you the kind of peace, wisdom, strength and deliverance that can only come from Him. David, once again sought the Lord, but even before he sought an answer about his present circumstances the Bible says "he found strength in the Lord his God." There will be times in our lives where we desperately need answers and David has given us a great model of prayer and worship. By first finding strength in the Lord, He gained the clarity to once again make sound decisions.

He then asked the Lord two questions. First, do you want me to go after them? And second, if you want me to go, will I win? You'll find The Lord's answer in 1 Samuel 30:8. "Pursue them," He answered. "You will certainly overtake them and succeed in the rescue." That's all David needed. God's promise. God's word. His strength was renewed and his confidence rebuilt. He gathered his mighty men for the rescue mission. With their adrenaline flowing the 600 men set out to take back what the enemy had stolen. Exhausted, yes. Emotionally spent, absolutely. So much so that 200 hundred of them had to stay back when they came to the Besor Valley. Yet verse 10 says, "But David and the other four hundred continued the pursuit."

As they were quickly gaining on the enemy they found an Egyptian slave of one of the Amalekites who had become ill and was tossed aside and left for dead. David and his men gave him food and water and revived him. David asked him if he could lead them to the enemy. After making a pact with David that he would not be returned to his old master, the slave gave David the location of the enemy.

He led David down, and there they were, scattered over the countryside, eating, drinking and reveling because of the great amount of plunder they had taken from the land of the Philistines and from Judah. David fought them from dusk until the evening of the next day, and none of them got away, except four hundred young men who rode off on camels and fled.

David had a score to settle. No one was coming into his home and taking his wife and children. This was an abduction and David would not tolerate it. David and his men engaged in battle from the dusk of one day into the evening of the next, and during the battle not a single man of David's was lost. All of the Amalekites were destroyed except 400 young men who fled away on camels.

1 Samuel 30, 18-19 are two of my favorite verses in the bible:

David recovered all that the Amalekites had taken and rescued his two wives. Nothing was missing, small or great, sons or daughters, spoil or anything that had been taken; David recovered all.

Even though David had drifted from God for awhile and it looked like all was lost, he remembered from where his help would come and he surrendered to his God. Look deeply at verse 19. "Nothing was missing, small or great, sons or daughters, spoil or anything that had been taken; David recovered all."

Nothing was missing. David recovered all. David recovered all. David recovered all. Restitution! He was fully restored.

David recovered all. Restitution! He was fully restored.

I love Isaiah 61. One of my favorite chapters in the entire bible. Look at it:

> The Spirit of the Sovereign LORD is on me, because the LORD has anointed me to proclaim good news to the poor. He has sent me to bind up the brokenhearted, to proclaim freedom for the captives and release from darkness for the prisoners, to proclaim the year of the LORD's favor and the day of vengeance of our God, to comfort all who mourn, and provide for those who grieve in Zion—to bestow on them a crown of beauty instead of ashes, the oil of joy instead of mourning, and a garment of praise instead of a spirit of despair.
>
> They will be called oaks of righteousness, a planting of the LORD for the display of his splendor. They will rebuild the ancient ruins and restore the places long devastated; they will renew the ruined cities that have been devastated for generations. Strangers will shepherd your flocks; foreigners will work your fields and vineyards.
>
> And you will be called priests of the LORD; you will be named ministers of our God. You will feed on the wealth of nations, and in their riches you will boast. Instead of your shame you will receive a double portion, and instead of disgrace you will rejoice in your inheritance. And so you will inherit a double portion in your land, and everlasting joy will be yours.
>
> "For I, the LORD, love justice; I hate robbery and wrongdoing. In my faithfulness I will reward my people and make an everlasting covenant with them. Their descendants

will be known among the nations and their offspring among the peoples. All who see them will acknowledge that they are a people the LORD has blessed." I delight greatly in the LORD; my soul rejoices in my God. For he has clothed me with garments of salvation and arrayed me in a robe of his righteousness, as a bridegroom adorns his head like a priest, and as a bride adorns herself with her jewels. For as the soil makes the sprout come up and a garden causes seeds to grow, so the Sovereign LORD will make righteousness and praise spring up before all nations.

Preaching good news to the poor. Healing the brokenhearted. Freedom for the captives. Bestowing joy instead of despair. The ruins in our lives can be repaired and restored. Even if they've been destroyed for generations, they can be rebuilt! We'll feed on the wealth of nations. No more shame and disgrace, but a double portion of our inheritance can be ours. Clothed in salvation. Covered in righteousness. Everlasting joy! That's my God!

David had a choice and so do you. When you face adversity do you sit on your hands and let a holocaust take over your home, or do you find strength and answers from the Lord. That's a choice you'll have to make and the decision will determine your destiny.

I can't promise you that you'll recover all. But with God nothing is impossible and He is the God of another chance. Be confident in this, He's longing for a relationship with you to show you what He's capable of doing, and restoring your joy. Whatever your families situation, surrender it completely to Him now. You must choose as David does, to take up the fight. There was a battle that had to be fought to restore what once was. There will be that same type battle if you want restoration to your marriage also. David's was an all night and all day sword fight. Yours won't be with a physical sword, but will need to be with a spiritual sword called the Word of God.

There will always be a battle because we are in a spiritual war with an enemy that is always lurking and waiting for you as husbands and fathers to take your eyes off your most precious possessions, so they can sneak in and rob and destroy. You can't be like those who throughout history have refused to step into your God given authority because it might get a little uncomfortable or messy. If all you do is sit on your hands and do very little or nothing, those actions or lack thereof will ultimately create your future, filled with regrets.

Remember the words of English philosopher Edmund Burke who said, "The only thing necessary for the triumph of evil is for good men to do nothing."

You have two choices men. Turn a deaf ear and hope it resolves itself or be men of action. Today, resolve that your call is to be a Man of Standing.

Today, determine that becoming a force of men, means, resources, wealth, virtue, valor, and ability is the priority in your manhood. That to pamper, protect, provide and pursue your wife is the priority in your marriage. With a tenacity that cannot be quenched decide to be like David who was a man after God's own heart, and make that the priority of your soul. But most of all, have a divine relationship with God through His Son and come onto the scene as an heir of the Most High God, and begin to reign in this life. Creation is waiting for it and so is your wife.

David recovered all that the Amalekites had taken…Nothing was missing, small or great, sons or daughters, spoil or anything that had been taken; David recovered all. May that be said of all Men of Standing.

CHAPTER 9

FULLY PERSUADED

N ow the LORD was gracious to Sarah as he had said, and
the LORD did for Sarah what he had promised. Sarah
became pregnant and bore a son to Abraham in his old
age, at the very time God had promised him. Abraham gave the name
Isaac to the son Sarah bore him. When his son Isaac was eight days
old, Abraham circumcised him, as God commanded him. Abraham
was a hundred years old when his son Isaac was born to him.

Sarah said, "God has brought me laughter, and everyone who
hears about this will laugh with me." And she added, "Who would
have said to Abraham that Sarah would nurse children? Yet I have
borne him a son in his old age."

Seven simple verses. If you never knew the story and just picked
up reading it here, it's one of many Old Testament stories with a

promise fulfilled. Look at the richness of the promises fulfilled. God was gracious to Sarah *as He had said*. He did for Sarah *what He had promised!* Sarah bore a son *at the very time God had promised him*. And Sarah said that *God has brought me laughter*. What a great story. God honored His word. But if you knew the account and the 24 years that it took to get this baby born, you would better understand the mercy and grace of a loving God, and the patience and perseverance of a God called man.

Abram is 75 years old when he arrives in the land of Canaan with his 65 year old wife Sarah who has been barren all her life. No children. No legacy to pass on. No joy or laughter from a newborn that all the other women were experiencing. It can be devastating. At the very least it certainly can be depressing. I know. My wife and I have been there. Liz and I went through 7 years of infertility treatments, testing, drugs, and surgeries. All to no avail. Every Mother's day there were tears. Every Father's day there was frustration.

> *Every Mother's day there were tears. Every Father's day there was frustration. Every baby dedication day at church was such a painful reminder, we wished we had stayed home.*

Every baby dedication day at church was such a painful reminder, we wished we had stayed home. The great news is God blessed us with 3 miracle babies. But we went through 7 years of struggles to get there. I can't imagine going through that for 70 years, but that's what Abram and Sarah did. And then God shows up one day and drops a bombshell on the two of them.

So Abram went, as the LORD had told him; and Lot went with him. Abram was seventy-five years old when he set out from Harran. He took his wife Sarai, his nephew Lot, all the possessions they had accumulated and the people they had acquired in Harran, and they set out for the land of Canaan, and they arrived there.

Abram traveled through the land as far as the site of the great tree of Moreh at Shechem. At that time the Canaanites were in the land. "To your offspring I will give this land." So he built an altar there to the LORD, who had appeared to him. (Genesis 12:1-6)

I don't know about you, but if the God of the universe tells me that my offspring are going to rule, I would be pretty excited. But not by the ruling, but merely because I'm going to have offspring! If I found out I was going to have children after decades of barrenness, I'm going to tell everyone I can, as loud as I can that we're about to have a baby. I don't care even if I was in my 70's there's going to be a shout, a handstand, a cartwheel, a marching band, something loud to celebrate with. But Abram just quietly builds an alter to the Lord. That's in chapter 12 and it isn't until chapter 15 and who knows how much time had passed that the bible even mentions his offspring again.

Worry had set in because of the delay in the birth and Abram was concerned that someone else would have to carry on other than his offspring. But that night God told Abram to look up and try and count the stars, because that was how numerous his offspring would be. In verse 6 Abram did something simple yet sometimes so difficult for us, and it forever changed his life, destiny, and eternity. He believed God. He took God at his word. What a novel idea! He just believed what God said and it was credited to him as righteousness. Was he then perfect? No. Did he still sin? Absolutely. As a matter of fact there's about to be a big screw up, and it's going to change the face of the world forever. But on that night, with that promise from the Lord, Abram believed God.

Ten years pass. No baby yet but offspring are mentioned again. But this time it's not from God or even Abram. It's from Sarah, and she is at her boiling point. You can hear it in her voice. Remember, they're very wealthy now partly because of her being given over by her husband to Pharaoh so Abram could save his skin. Sarah's probably heard all she wants to hear about these future miracle offspring, and she's ready for some results. So she says, "The Lord has kept me from having children. Go, sleep with my slave; perhaps I can build a family through her." Three statements leave her mouth. None are from God. First she plays the blame game. She actually blames God for her not having children. The Bible is not clear about her specific issue, and I wasn't there, but I can promise you that her barrenness wasn't from God. There's a ton of other reasons that can cause a barren womb, but one thing is for sure, God isn't punishing her because it was His will was for her and Abram to have children. Second, she turns the tables on Abram. Instead of Abram giving her over to Pharaoh for his pleasure and for Abrams profit, she now gives Abram over to her slave girl for Sarah's benefit.

For whatever reason Abram has lost his manhood and he's now in the passenger seat. Maybe the guilt from his actions in Egypt years ago resurfaced. Maybe she's been nagging for so long it's taken its toll. We're not sure what all took place, but it's clear that Sarah is now calling the shots. She's angry, and like we all do at different times in our lives she's letting circumstances drive her decisions and not God. It makes sense to her, but that's because she is thinking with her senses and not the Spirit. She might have thought, "He threw me into a sexual pit so he could get what he wanted and now it's my turn. I want a baby. Go have sex with my maid Hagar." And Abram did so. No debate, no argument from Abram at all. The slippery slope just became an all out fall off the cliff because as soon as he has sex with her and she becomes pregnant, Sarah begins to despise her. Shocker! She gives her husband to another woman and now she has to listen and watch as Hagar is pregnant and she's still not.

But look at the last thing Sarah said. "Perhaps *I can build* a family through her!" I can see this conversation between the two. Abram is standing there looking like someone had just run over his favorite puppy with a chariot. Shoulders slumped. No eye contact with Sarah. Totally deflated and his wife is basically telling him to his face that he's not man enough, and he can't get the job done even though she was the one who was barren. "God, you haven't done it yet so let me have a turn. I'll take over from here and I'll get it done."

We've all done it. We've got ahead of God. We think that if we take matters into our hands we can do it better. But it always backfires. She tells Abram to have sex with Hagar. Hagar gets pregnant. Welcome Ishmael. And then it seems to get real quiet between God and Abram.

The next verse starts off with, "When Abram was 99 years old the Lord appeared to him and said I am God Almighty; walk before me faithfully and be blameless."

Do the math. That's 13 years later. Nothing recorded in the Bible for all that time! Wonder what the communication was like between God and Abram all those years. A lot? None? I'm convinced it was somewhere between the two, but one thing is for sure. Nothing of significance in this miracle baby story has taken place, until God shows up.

The Lord shows up and makes a covenant with Abram. He said, "Walk before me faithfully and be blameless. Then I will make my covenant between me and you and will greatly increase your numbers."

Abram fell facedown, and God said to him, "As for me, this is my covenant with you: You will be the father of many nations. No longer will you be called Abram; your name will be Abraham, for I have made you a father of many nations. I will make you very fruitful; I will make nations of you, and kings will come from you. I will establish my covenant as an everlasting covenant between me and you and your descendants after you for the generations to come, to be your God and the God of your descendants after you. The whole land of Canaan, where you now reside as a foreigner, I will give as an everlasting possession to you and your descendants after you; and I will be their God."

Then God said to Abraham, "As for you, you must keep my covenant, you and your descendants after you for the generations to come. This is my covenant with you and your descendants after you, the covenant you are to keep: Every male among you shall be circumcised. You are to undergo circumcision, and it will be the sign of the covenant between me and you. For the generations to come every male among you who is eight days old must be circumcised, including those born in your household or bought with money from a foreigner—those who are not your offspring. Whether born in your household or bought with your money, they must be circumcised. My covenant in your flesh is to be an everlasting covenant. Any uncircumcised male, who has not been circumcised in the flesh, will be cut off from his people; he has broken my covenant."

God also said to Abraham, "As for Sarai your wife, you are no longer to call her Sarai; her name will be Sarah. I will bless her and will surely give you a son by her. I will bless her so that she will be the mother of nations; kings of peoples will come from her."

Abraham fell facedown; he laughed and said to himself, "Will a son be born to a man a hundred years old? Will Sarah bear a child at the age of ninety?" And Abraham said to God, "If only Ishmael might live under your blessing!"

Then God said, "Yes, but your wife Sarah will bear you a son, and you will call him Isaac. I will establish my covenant with him as an everlasting covenant for his descendants after him. And as for Ishmael, I have heard you: I will surely bless him; I will make him fruitful and will greatly increase his numbers. He will be the father of twelve rulers, and I will make him into a great nation. But my covenant I will establish with Isaac, whom Sarah will bear to you by this time next year." When he had finished speaking with Abraham, God went up from him.

Here's my take. God shows up and says, "Okay, are the two of you finally ready to listen? I watched as you settled in Haran wasting time for years. A place I never intended you to settle in. I carefully protected you and guided you from the Ur of the Chaldeans into the land of Canaan so you would worship me because I have an incredible plan for your life. I've seen your worry. I have heard your complaints and I witnessed your mistake with Hagar. Now that a little time has past I think I have your attention."

And a gracious God laid out a covenant that He made with Abram as to the greatness of His name, and to Sarah becoming fertile at a ripe old age. God continues:

"Abraham, kings will come from you. Nations will be born from you. I'm making you extremely fruitful. You're going to have a son. His name is Isaac and an everlasting covenant will be between you and me. That's my part! Incredible! Absolutely amazing! Greater than anything you could ever ask or imagine. As for your name Abram which means exalted father, I'm changing it to Abraham, meaning father of a multitude. That will best describe your new life. Here's your part of the covenant. You need to circumcise yourself. Not only yourself but every boy and man in your household."

I'm sure it's at this point that there is some rather lengthy dialogue between Abraham and God about this issue of circumcision. We read that "Abraham circumcised himself and everybody in his household," and don't think much of it, but it had never been done before. Stop and think about what He's requiring Abraham to do! If I'm Abraham, it's at this point once I fully understand what I've just been asked to do that I might try and negotiate with the Lord. How about if my part is to fast for 7 days? How about I sacrifice a really big bull? Shave my beard? Paint my toenails? Something else Lord because…can you imagine what I'm going to have to tell my men that work for me? Okay guys, I've got some good news…and some bad news. The good news is that we're all going to be a part of a great nation and be blessed beyond our wildest dreams! The bad news is you're going to have to drop your loin cloth for a slight surgical procedure! I thought I had it rough when my mom made me get a flu shot for the school.

> *The good news is that we're all going to be a part of a great nation and be blessed beyond our wildest dreams! The bad news is you're going to have to drop your loin cloth for a slight surgical procedure!*

Think about what must have been going through Abrahams mind. "You want me to what, and then you want me to do what with Sarah?" Is it even going to work after this self induced surgery you're asking me to perform? I've never been to medical school Lord and this is one procedure that I really don't want to mess up on! I mean if I cut myself shaving then it's okay but this …? But Abraham doesn't flinch or try to negotiate. This is what I think. He knew that he had blown it several times, and for many years, and I believe that he realized that it was never meant to take this long to have a son, but there were things that both Abraham and Sarah empowered and allowed to get in the way. This time Abraham didn't stutter, sputter, or limp. He received his instructions and on how to do the procedure, and the Bible says that very day every man, boy, and Abraham himself was circumcised. There was no delay. There was no worrying. There was no argument, and there was no substitution for the commitment.

Sometime later on three supernatural visitors, including the Lord came to spend a little time with Abraham and Sarah, and told them that in about a year He would come back and Sarah would have a son. She laughed to herself and thought, "After I am worn out and my lord is old, will I now have this pleasure?" But the Lord hears everything and He heard her laugh and her thoughts to herself. He asked Abraham a very powerful question. "Is anything too hard for the Lord?"

Let me ask us all the same question. Is anything too hard for the Lord? Is anything to hard for the Lord? As good little Christians we'd all sanctimoniously answer, "Why no of course not Jesus!" I'm going to ask it one more time. Is anything too hard for the Lord? Your truthful answer will define your destiny.

Can my marriage be renewed? Can my dreams become reality? Can my finances be restored? Fill in your own blanks, but know this: there is nothing, absolutely nothing too hard for the Lord. Abraham was 99. Sarah was 90 and barren. But God was God then and He is still the same God today!

So where are you with your miracle? We each have dreams and desires. Maybe you have a revelation that God showed you once by peeling back the curtain of the future and letting you see your dream. Where are you with your miracle, and better yet, what are you doing while you wait for it to appear? I want to give you a couple of thoughts and a several verses to help us all in our walk and sometimes in our wait.

First, I'm going to blow some of your theology out of the water. We hear it in church all the time. "Our timing, is not God's timing." I agree. I believe many times God's timing is faster than ours! Let that one sink in.

Sarah was barren! It didn't matter if she was 21, 51, 91, or 121. She was barren and a baby born from a barren womb is a miracle, period! God had a miracle for them but it wasn't going to take place while they were worshiping idols in the Ur of the Chaldeans, and it wasn't going to happen when they settled in Haran. It was going to take place in Canaan, the land of miracles. Here's my first question. How long has it been since the Lord gave you a revelation of something you were to accomplish, but instead of immediately getting it done you settled in your own Haran? Abraham might have been there 40 years. We don't know, but what we do know is that it was never God's will for him to settle anywhere other than Canaan.

Second, going down to Egypt and handing his wife over to Pharaoh as a plaything? We've already covered that in chapter 3, but how long could that have pushed back their miracle? Third, How much delay was caused by all the worrying over God's promises like Abraham did in chapter 15; and agreeing to have a child with Hagar? More delay? But it seems that when God finally gets their undivided attention, He shows up with a name and date for their miracle.

Let me give you two scriptures to back that up.

I am the LORD your God, who brought you up out of Egypt. Open wide your mouth and I will fill it "But my people would not listen to me; Israel would not submit to me. So I gave them over to their stubborn hearts to follow their own devices. "If my people would only listen to me, if Israel would only follow my ways, how *quickly* I would subdue their enemies and turn my hand against their foes! Those who hate the LORD would cringe before him, and their punishment would last forever. But you would be fed with the finest of wheat; with honey from the rock I would satisfy you." (Psalms 81:10-16)

Open wide your mouths. Fully surrender to the love of God. Listen to Him and surrender to Him. Look at verse 14. I will slowly subdue your enemies? No, quickly! God wants to quickly subdue your enemies. Those things that stand between you and the promises He has made to you He wants to remove immediately. Let that verse sink in and renew your mind about the love of God. He's not some evil father dangling your dreams and needs over your head while laughing. He's your loving Heavenly Father who longs to quickly come to the rescue to His children. Open wide your mouths.

"Hope deferred makes the heart sick, but a longing fulfilled is a tree of life!" (Proverbs 13:12)

Do you think God wants to have a bunch of sick kids with broken hearts? Absolutely not! But that's what deferred hope does. Men, we've been lied to. I believe our loving Heavenly Father wants to bless us more than we can imagine. He wants to give it to us a lot quicker than we think He does. What fulfilled Adam and Eve in the garden? It was the Tree of Life. God wanted them to partake of it and the same holds true today. God wants our longings He gives us to be fulfilled because to us it's a tree of life! It's health. It's abundance. It's His will!

So what do we do when we're faced with a delay in our dreams? There are things that just take time. Pregnancies take nine months. Education takes a few years. There will be some times for whatever reason, be it God's will or our delay, that waiting will have to occur. What do we do then? Abraham gave us a beautiful picture once the Lord gave him a name and a date.

As it is written: "I have made you a father of many nations." He is our father in the sight of God, in whom he believed—the God who gives life to the dead and calls into being things that were not.

Against all hope, Abraham in hope believed and so became the father of many nations, just as it had been said to him, "So shall your offspring be." Without weakening in his faith, he faced the fact that his body was as good as dead—since he was about a hundred years old—and that Sarah's womb was also dead. Yet he did not waver through unbelief regarding the promise of God, but was strengthened in his faith and gave glory to God, being fully persuaded that God had power to do what he had promised. (Romans 4:17-22)

Notice this all happened after God showed with a name and a date. It wasn't when they first arrived in Canaan and God told them they would have offspring. Look at the verse again. Without weakening in his faith, he faced the fact that his body was as good as dead—since he was about a *hundred years old*—and that Sarah's womb was also dead. This was all after He got their attention.

There were 7 things Abraham did that were keys to his success and his peace of mind and, they still serve as a great model of faith for us today.

Against all hope, Abraham in hope believed. Even though the circumstances around him were screaming, "No hope!" Abraham decided to act in hope, and he believed that what God said was more powerful than what the circumstances were. Today, if you're in the midst of what seems like no hope, invite the God of all hope into your circumstances and let Him take control.

He refused to weaken in his faith. Regardless how many times that bad movie played in Abraham's mind that it was never going to happen, he refused to weaken in his faith. He kept renewing his mind with God's spoken word and the same holds true today. There are 66 books in the bible filled to overflowing with promises from God to His children. Find several and write them on the doors of your heart and see what God can do. Even if you have to speak them out loud several times a day, do so until they replace the thoughts from the enemy with the mind of Christ.

He didn't walk around in denial, acting like the circumstances weren't real. He faced his circumstances. He knew they were real. He just didn't empower them or give them any authority in his life by believing in them. Faced them? Yes. Empowered them? No. Just like David did with Goliath. He didn't act like the giant wasn't standing there. He just refused to give him any authority in his life. He didn't wilt at his size. He just told him his God was much bigger than he was, and he went out and showed Goliath just how big God is.

He did not waiver in unbelief regarding the promise of God. He didn't wake up one day and believe and then next day wake up and falter. He was consistently unwavering in his trust in God. Remember Peter getting out of the boat and walking on water? So long as he kept his eyes on Jesus he defied gravity. But when the wind and waves caused him to look at them instead of Jesus he sank. Keep your eyes on Jesus and walk in victory. Begin to look at circumstances and empower them and our walking on water quickly becomes an unpleasant swim.

He was strengthened and bolstered by his faith. He remembered all the times that God had proven himself faithful throughout all the years since he had arrived in Canaan. It's good to revisit the times in our lives where God came through in difficult or seemingly impossible situations. It strengthens us because we are reminded that He can do it all again.

He gave glory to God. In those quiet moments of prayer and reflection he gave glory to God. He worshipped. He sang. He knew that this miracle would only come from his Heavenly Father and he gave him all the glory. The Bible says the Lord inhabits the praises of His people. He gets right in the middle of those praises and camps with us. In our lives, the battle might look like it's was won on the battlefield, but I believe that the outcome was determined during those times of worship and praise.

He was fully persuaded. He had heard the voice of God and he left no room in his mind for any doubt. He refused to empower doubt, and he became the father of many nations.

Today you might be facing what appear to be some pretty insurmountable odds. Isaiah 51 says to look at the example that Abraham gave us. When God first called him he was only one man, but God blessed him. In spite of all Abraham's mistakes and screw ups God was faithful and kept His promises. He was then and He still is today. The Word says to look to Jesus, the author, writer, and creator of our faith. And He is also the one who perfects it and completes it.

One of my absolute favorite verses is Romans 8:31-32. It says, "What, then, shall we say in response to these things? If God is for us, who can be against us? He who did not spare his own Son, but gave him up for us all—how will he not also, along with him, graciously give us all things?"

God gave us his absolute best when He freely gave us Jesus. He has not stopped giving us His absolute best. Open your mouth wide and receive all that God wants to do in your life and your circumstances, and become fully persuaded!

FOR LADIES ONLY

Know your audience. That's rule number one in public speaking. Know their hot buttons. Know what moves them. Know what they want to hear. Know what they need to hear, but be wise. Know what you can and cannot say. Over the years I've given countless speeches to educators across the country. Superintendents, school boards, teachers and parents and the one thing you always know is that you could never stand before that group and talk God or politics. In today's educational systems that's a great way to have your speech come to an abrupt halt. But possessing my lifelong anti-establishment sense of humor I sometimes wanted to be introduced by the announcer, walk up to the podium and say, "God is a Republican!" Just to see how riled up I could get them. Just by saying that I've probably wrinkled a few feathers of some readers.

Ease up on the frustration meter dude. He's neither Republican nor Democrat. He's King. He owns it all and makes all the rules and every one of them is perfect and for the betterment of His children.

The same holds true with writing a book. Know your reader! All you have to do is look online and you'll find that women buy more books than men and also read more than men. So why am I boring you with these facts? Because of this chapter. This one is for the ladies. There are 11 chapters in this book. Most are directly speaking to men, but this one is for the females. It's going to be just as true, but a tad more sensitive than the others. I know who's going to be reading this. Whether it's a wife who buys this for her husband and reads it first, or if it's a husband who buys this and gives this chapter to his wife to read is irrelevant. What is relevant is that it's read just like the others; with an open heart and a will to change anything that has to be changed. So please ladies, just as the other chapters serve as a roadmap to spiritual manhood being healed, renewed, and unleashed so too this chapter is geared at seeing you healed and renewed so that your inner and outer beauty, that was wonderfully created by a loving God, will be unleashed into your own life and into the lives of your husband and family like never before.

One disclaimer before we get going. There are millions of marriages with each one being at a different level. Some are great. Most need help. Some are in drastic need of counseling because of abuse. Never put or keep yourself in danger. This chapter is for the vast majority that is safe yet in need of help.

I heard a story about a lady who went to the doctor with sharp pains all over her body. She sat in the examination room with her physician and described her pain. She would take her right index finger and touch her left knee, and would scream out in pain. Then she'd take the same finger and touch her right ankle and again would scream out because of the incredibly sharp pain. Again and again she would take her finger and touch places all over her body, with the same resulting pain. Her back, shoulders, both sides of her jaw, wherever she touched there was pain. After an extensive exam and subsequent set of x-rays the doctor looked her square in the face and said, "Lady, you have a broken right index finger!"

And there is the lesson for this chapter. Everyone carries a source of pain. Some are microscopic. Some are enormous. All you have to do is be around someone for awhile and you'll usually be able to tell the level of pain that is radiating through them. Many times the pain that seems to radiate all over your life can be traced to one specific cause.

There are many origins of pain. A relationship that went south. A tragic event in a person's life. Too many to count. But there is one that I want to focus on for this chapter because I believe it's at the very root for many who have suffered with hurt that seemingly never goes away in their lives. It's the pain of fatherlessness.

Decades of research show that when a dad leaves, kids lose. Tonight in this great nation approximately 40% of children will go to bed in a house without their natural father, and in the African American community that figure is as much as 70% or more. Research shows that kids without the benefit of a connected father both physically and emotionally are more susceptible to deep poverty, lower grades, low self esteem, promiscuity, drug activity, gang involvement, depression, and higher rates of suicide.

There was a study done based on 17,000 children born in the United Kingdom in 1958. These children were followed up by the researchers at ages 7, 11, 16, 23 and at 33 years of age. Several startling statistics were found, but for this chapter here's your finding. The females in the research group who had a strong relationship with their father as they were growing up "showed a lack of psychological distress in their adult lives."

One more undeniable piece of research. God said it. It's the very last words in the very last book in the Old Testament. He said He would send Elijah and he would turn the hearts of the fathers to their children and the hearts of the children to their fathers, or else there would be a curse on the land. Think poverty, promiscuity, violence, depression, and suicide aren't a curse? It's happened because of the fatherlessness world we live in, and it causes untold pain in the lives of adults and children.

And this curse of fatherlessness crosses all lines of race, religion, cultures, and economic levels. I've witnessed it in some of the poorest areas of our nation, where a dad followed in his father's footsteps and left the mother of his children with the same attitude as he would quit a job he didn't like. I've also seen fatherlessness in some of the richest areas of our country, where a father would fly out for business meetings on Monday, get back late Friday, more meetings in the office on Saturday and golf on Sunday with the boys at the club. It's an epidemic. It's everywhere and Men of Standing need to rise up and cause it to become a thing of the past.

But many of you ladies already know this hurt and you must confront it and deal with it, or like the lady with the broken index finger everything and everyone you touch will be affected by the damage that you've experienced. You may think it's your husband or your kids that makes you miserable, but I challenge you to dig deep, deeper than you've ever gone before and rid yourself of this issue that causes you such grief.

You start this healing process by forgiving him. Your father left you when you needed him most, you forgive him. He never told you that you were beautiful, you forgive him. He never told you he loved you, you forgive him. He cheated on your family, you forgive him. I'll stop right there. Whatever the vice, forgive him. Release him from your bitterness. Release him from your hurts. Release him over to the Heavenly Father who specializes in repairing hearts and relationships, and let Him take control of the issue even if your father is no longer alive. If you choose not to, you set yourself up for more suffering for you and your family, and it will come in many forms.

Let me share one common form. You develop a fierce spirit of independence. He left me. He didn't connect or communicate to me. I guess I'll just have to do this myself. Get out of the way world, I'll get the job done. It's great to be passionate, but it's painful for all of your family for you to possess a strong sense of independence. The great grandson of Adam that you married, who is already inclined to be passive and quiet during times of stress, will only empower you to lord over him even more and for him to cower even deeper. It's a dangerous cycle. Forgive. Maybe it wasn't your father. Maybe it was or is your husband. The same healing remedy holds true and it starts with forgiveness.

There may need to be counseling or other types of specialized help. There are pastors, counselors, books, all kinds of resources; but somewhere in the healing equation complete forgiveness needs to be settled. If not, no other specialized help with work, and will end in frustration and more pain for your family.

No doubt this entire book is written to men and how we can throw off all the Clark Kent clothes that weigh us down in order that we might truly become the husband of your dreams. But there is still a huge responsibility that you bare. It's not the sole responsibility of your husband to make you happy, bring you peace or meet your every need. You have responsibilities too. Starting with loving yourself, so you can be lovable to him and your children. Finding happiness and peace within? You own those too. And just like I have clearly said to the men, all of this will be found in a Heavenly Father who is radically pursuing you so you can find and know Him. You need to experience His unfailing and unconditional love for you on a daily basis so in turn you can express that love to your husband and family. All along He's been waiting on you to come to Him for your healing and your restoration. He is waiting on you now.

> *Starting with loving yourself, so you can be lovable to him and your children.*

As men we looked at Boaz as a model, but as I read through Ruth again, especially the first 3 chapters, I find several life changing actions that Ruth chose that ultimately brought her the man of her dreams.

First, even after all the hurt and loss she sustained in her life she was willing to leave her homeland and make the God of Naomi, the one true God, her own God. Orpah, Ruth's sister-in-law chose to stay in Moab and worship foreign gods but Ruth chose to leave her family, heritage, and her comfort zone and travel this new path.

At this they wept aloud again. Then Orpah kissed her mother-in-law goodbye, but Ruth clung to her.

"Look," said Naomi, "your sister-in-law is going back to her people and her gods. Go back with her."

But Ruth replied, "Don't urge me to leave you or to turn back from you. Where you go I will go, and where you stay I will stay. Your people will be my people and your God my God."

Ruth had a passion to find God. Despite her upbringing, despite her past beliefs she had a passion for Naomi's God. Ladies, find a passion in your relationship with God like never before, and let that passion flow into your relationship with your husband, regardless of where he is in his own walk with the Lord. Pray for him daily. Pray with him often. Even if he's distant. Even if he seems to not care. Let him see this passion in you for God.

Next, Ruth spoke blessings back to Boaz. Ruth 2:13 says, "May I continue to find favor in your eyes, my lord," she said. "You have put me at ease by speaking kindly to your servant—though I do not have the standing of one of your servants."

Now I know there's going to be some who say, "Yeah, it's easy to talk that way to your husband if he'll do for me what Boaz did for her!" I get that. But why not start talking to him in the way you want to be talked to, and plant that seed in him and see what kind of harvest you get back. Plant seeds of complaint and guess what you will harvest? Plant seeds of love and kindness and encouragement and see what happens over time! Ruth could have said, "Well it's about time you noticed my hard work!" But she didn't. She chose kindness. Kindness like so many other vital components that make an incredible marriage is a choice. Ruth chose wisely and it paid great dividends for her for years to come. Choose wisely.

Next, Ruth rediscovered her passion for marriage. Ruth had suffered loss. All marriages can suffer some type of loss at one time or another. Maybe not a physical loss but an emotional loss. A romantic loss. A friendship loss. There are many. But Ruth found her passion again and it breathed new life into her soul.

Why doesn't the passion last? Why does the honeymoon wear off? Remember back to those first few months and years? Where did they go? I'm going to give you a possible answer as an analogy. We treat our spouse like a pair of shoes. All nice and shiny when they're brand new. But after we wear them a few times they get a scratched here and there. Forget to polish them or take good care of them and all of a sudden they're on the back of the shelf. We get used to each other. We get a little too comfortable around each other and lose that intimacy. Life and marriage becomes routine. There are a million possible reasons why a marriage might grow dull, but here's my number one belief on why it does.

We lose the honeymoon effect because the world tells us we're supposed to! We're told, "It's never supposed to last!" Let that sink in ladies! Ask any human being if the honeymoon is supposed to last forever. Almost everyone will say no. Why? Who said so? Who made that rule? Answer this. If keeping the honeymoon going was a top priority for both of you, do you think it could happen? Before you say no answer this. You have a priority to eat and you do that rather well don't you? Many of you make it a priority to hit the gym and stay in shape don't you? Have kids? Own a home? Pay a huge mortgage? Own at least two cars? Every member of the family has a cell phone don't they? We do a million things a day because they are part of our lives. They are our daily choices we make because they seem to be what we are supposed to do. We make them all a priority. But let someone tell you that

> *We lose the honeymoon effect because the world tells us we're supposed to!*

you're supposed to keep the honeymoon alive and active and we think it's impossible because the world around us keeps telling us it is. It's a mindset! I can promise you the pain and suffering in the modern day marriage would become a microscopic if we all made it a priority to keep the honeymoon alive. We do what we do and we think what we think

We do what we do and we think what we think because someone told us that's the way it should be, but what if their way is wrong? What if we bought into an error?

because someone told us that's the way it should be, but what if their way is wrong? What if we bought into an error? Right now you're saying, "It's impossible!" Really? Why?

Is our relationship with God supposed to become old and worn out, or does He desire for us to be renewed in our minds each day so that we can experience a deeper level of intimacy with Him? What do you think would happen if you and your closest friends made a covenant with each other to rediscover the passion of your marriage and it worked? Then all your friends would be looking at you and they would want to know what you discovered. And it's not a pill. It's called a revolution. Jude Wanniski was quoted in his book, *The Way the World Works* as saying:

"It is in the nature of revolution, the overturning of the existing order, that in it's inception a very small number of people are involved. The process in fact, begins with one person as an idea, an idea that persuades a second, then a third and a fourth, and gathers force until the idea is successfully contradicted, absorbed into conventional wisdom, or actually turns the world upside down. A revolution requires not only ammunition, but also weapons and men willing to use them and willing to be slain in the battle. In an intellectual revolution, there must be ideas and advocates willing to challenge an entire profession, the establishment itself, willing to spend their reputations and careers in spreading the idea through deeds as well as words."

Are you ready for a rebirth of passion? I am. I want that in my own marriage. I say it can be done. I'll be the pioneer. Are you willing to believe and follow?

Fourth, she knew how to catch her man. I love this part of the story. Most men do too. Naomi instructs Ruth on how to attract Boaz to her. Chapter 3 starts off by saying:

One day Ruth's mother-in-law Naomi said to her, "My daughter, I must find a home for you, where you will be well provided for. Now Boaz, with whose women you have worked, is a relative of ours. Tonight he will be winnowing barley on the threshing floor. Wash, put on perfume, and get dressed in your best clothes. Then go down to the threshing floor, but don't let him know you are there until he has finished eating and drinking. When he lies down, note the place where he is lying. Then go and uncover his feet and lie down. He will tell you what to do."

Naomi is ready for Ruth to be taken care of and she knows just the strategy that will get Boaz's attention. It worked that night and it still works today. She told her to bathe, perfume from head to toe and put on the finest dress. Modern day translation, "Girl, you need to look and smell good!"

It's very easy to become comfortable in our appearance once we get married. I was getting my oil changed one time and one of the employees that was working on my car spilled some oil on himself and he just laughed and said, "Yeah, I'm married now so I don't have to worry about staying handsome and looking good for my ol' lady!" I just laughed to myself as about a thousand sarcastic comebacks flowed in my mind. This guy looked liked he couldn't even attract daylight. Greasy, grimy, sloppy, and looked like he hadn't seen a mirror in about a year. But I just kept my mouth shut and remembered that I was going to put that comment in this book.

A little time passes. The dress becomes a pair of baggy gym shorts and a t-shirt and the perfume is somewhere in the makeup drawer in your bathroom. Clearly hear me. No one is asking for perfection. Just once in a while dress and smell like you did on your first date with your husband. Do you remember when you wouldn't come to the door unless all your makeup was on? That still works today! And I know there is school stuff, soccer games, cooking, cleaning, and midnight feedings. No way in the world I'm minimizing any of these. Just surprise him sometimes when he least expects it with a pursuit that will cause him to remember those early moments when you were dating.

Last, Ruth Chapter 3 records the comment when Boaz was awakened by Ruth.

When Boaz had finished eating and drinking and was in good spirits, he went over to lie down at the far end of the grain pile. Ruth approached quietly, uncovered his feet and lay down. In the middle of the night something startled the man; he turned—and there was a woman lying at his feet! "Who are you?" he asked. "I am your servant Ruth," she said. "Spread the corner of your garment over me, since you are a guardian-redeemer of our family." "The LORD bless you, my daughter," he replied. "This kindness is greater than that which you showed earlier: You have not run after the younger men, whether rich or poor. And now, my daughter, don't be afraid. I will do for you all you ask. All the people of my town know that you are a woman of noble character.

Look again at the last line. "All the people of my town know you are a woman of noble character." The bible doesn't record how long Ruth had been in this town but regardless of the timeframe, she had made a name for herself with the community. The New American Standard Bible calls her a "woman of excellence" and the King James Version calls her "a "virtuous woman." Any way you shake it you are translating the word "chayil". Look familiar? It should. It's the same word translated for "standing!" A Man of Standing found his Woman of Standing.

I don't know what type of life Ruth lived before she found God on the road to Judah. Being from Moab chances are it wasn't the best. But one thing we know, she received the God of Abraham, Isaac, and Jacob when she said that Naomi's God would be her God and her life changed from that point and the blessings began to pour into her. Meeting God changed her eternity. Meeting Boaz changed her destiny.

Today, your husband might not be living as a Man of Standing, but it is my prayer for you that this chapter can be used by a loving God to heal you of any hurts that keeps your life in pain. That you can find and experience His love for you and His beautiful dreams for you; that in turn can unleash your inner beauty into you becoming the woman you've always dreamed of being. I pray that this transformation occurs in your life with such force that your husband and children see it, and begin to experience the love of the Father through you like never before. It can happen. Don't let the enemy tell you or convince you that it can't. He's the father of lies and he's just living out his character.

Jeremiah 33:3 says, "Call to me and I will answer you and tell you great and unsearchable things you do not know." Call out to Him. He's been waiting and he has incredible things He wants to do in your life and in the life of your family.

"Call to me and I will answer you and tell you great and unsearchable things you do not know." Call out to Him. He's been waiting and he has incredible things He wants to do in your life and in the life of your family.

Become a Woman of Standing and be a helpmate for your husband to become a Man of Standing! Imagine two forces with the same passion working as one for the good of their marriage and family! It will be something the world will line up to see.

CHAPTER 11

THE COVENANT
OF STANDING

I
t was a phone call no one would ever want to receive. It doesn't matter how Superman you are, this one was tough. It was excruciating. One of my closest friends was calling me to say goodbye. And I don't mean he was calling to tell me he was leaving to go back home from a trip. He was calling me to tell me he was going home for eternity.

Over the years this man had become one of my most trusted and closest friends. We possessed a unique relationship. There were times where he pushed me well beyond my comfort zone, and there were many times he and his family gave me great comfort. There were times I was so mad at him I didn't want to speak to him, but there were many more times during difficult and trying days that he was the only one I wanted to talk to. He was witty and humorous.

He was smart and he was balanced. He was a model to follow in his relationship with his wife and with his kids. At all times he wanted the best for me and my family. He made me a better man.

We had some intense meetings where we pushed and pulled at one another, all for the betterment of the organizations we ran. We had great times of fellowship where we thoroughly enjoyed each other's company. We laughed together, we planned together, we traveled together and we spoke together. But on that day that he called we cried together.

He had been suffering for months with several medical complications that attacked his body. After a time the doctors told him to go home, because there was nothing more they could do. He called me to say goodbye. I've never had a conversation quite like that one, and I never want to have another one like it again. I will always remember the instructions he gave me that day. With his weak, frail voice he told me to make sure Watch D.O.G.S. continues to get in as many schools as possible, and then he told me to make sure I take this mission called Man of Standing to the top. He knew this was my new calling. I left what I thought would be my mission for many years to come in order to write this book and begin a new chapter in my life, to reach men around the world with this Superman life and he was spurring me on, just like he had when we had worked side by side with Watch D.O.G.S. and The National Center for Fathering. I was crying like a baby as he lovingly gave me a few more final words from his heart, and then he said goodbye. Two days later he was gone. That day the world of fathering lost a great man. That day, Barb lost a great husband and Peter, Erin, Megan, Annie, Charlie, and Timmy lost a great dad.

Last words to family. Last words to friends. They're extremely intimate. They're of utmost priority. They are everything the person wants to say before they say goodbye.

Jesus shared those words the night before He was crucified to a small group of scared men. They would soon become revolutionists and take this carpenter from Galilee's message about the Kingdom of God to the world, and it continues its massive expansion around the globe 2000 years later. David spoke them into Solomon's life right before he died when he told his son, "Be strong, show yourself a man and do what the Lord requires." The word "strong" used here in the Hebrew is the word "chazaq" and it means "to strengthen, prevail, harden, be strong, become strong, be courageous, be firm, grow firm, be resolute, be sore." That's a man's man word; not an ounce of estrogen anywhere around it. It's a word that every man needs to have burned deep into his soul. It's a word that if we bring it into our lives and allow God to lead us, would completely reshape our mindset, our marriages, and our masculinity. It would utterly change our businesses as our boldness, courage, and resolute decision to succeed would dominate the competition. And yes, there would be soreness. You don't build muscle of any type without it but even in the growing pains of prevailing there would be a satisfaction that the workout is worth the reward. Solomon became "chazaq" and became the richest man in the history of the world. 2 Chronicles 1:1 it says, "Solomon son of David established himself firmly over his kingdom, for the Lord his God was with him and made him exceedingly great. The word "established" is the same word "chazaq" in Hebrew. Solomon followed his father's advice and built a kingdom like none other. But look at the next phrase. "For the Lord his God was with him and made him exceedingly great." There are two key components to this incredibly important verse about manhood. Solomon made a choice to man-up, and at the same time he allowed God to be God within him. God was with him and made him exceedingly great. Why? So Solomon could show off his financial muscle? No, He made him great so Solomon could show the world there is a God in the house of Israel. It's the same truth today. God is no respecter of persons. What He did for Solomon He can do for us. He can make your name great. He can build your business to heights you've never imagined and He can take your marriage to where you've only dreamed it. Why? So you can flex your muscle and bring glory to your flesh? No, so we can show the world what can happen when the willing vessel comes in contact with the loving God.

Moses penned the words of Deuteronomy. Some of his last words, written under the inspiration of the Holy Spirit on the east side of the Jordan River, just steps away from the Promised Land after leading the children of Israel for over four decades. After this 40 year journey God was ready for His children to enter into a land they couldn't even conceive in their minds. Peace awaited them along with abundance, prosperity, and rest. It was all created for them from the great love and the good pleasure of their Heavenly Father. All that stood between the end of the desert and the new beginnings of the Promised Land was a river to cross, and God stood ready to part the waters as He had done before as He watched and waited for them to activate their faith and rest in His word.

The same holds true for us today. In spite of what you may have been taught, there remains a life for each of God's children to enter into. A life beyond our comprehension. A life of blessings and prosperity. Protection and rest. Jesus called it "Zoe Perriso". The translators called it, "life and have it to the full." As good as

As Men of Standing, when our eyes are finally opened to the "confidence of our calling, the riches of His glorious inheritance and the incomparably great power to us who believe" as Ephesians 1 says, then we'll never be able to settle for anything less than "Zoe Perriso."

that translation sounds, it falls dramatically short of its true meaning. "Zoe" means the absolute fullness of life. A life real and genuine. Active and vigorous! "Perriso" means exceeding some number or measure or rank or need, over and above, more than is necessary, superadded…exceeding abundantly, supremely… something further, more, much more than all, and that's not even all the terms that translate this word! Believe it or not. Accept it or not that's the life that Jesus came to give to anyone who would receive it. And all that stands between the edge of the desert you currently stand in and the entrance into a John 10:10 destiny is a river to cross. But this Jordan is no actual river. This is a river of doubt and unbelief, religious mindsets and human error yet just like He did 3500 years ago the Creator of the universe stands ready for us to take Him at His word. As Men of Standing, when our eyes are finally opened to the "confidence of our calling, the riches of His glorious inheritance and the incomparably great power to us who believe" as Ephesians 1 says, then we'll never be able to settle for anything less than "Zoe Perriso."

Knowing this was his final opportunity to pour into his people Moses penned the final thoughts and commands given to him by God so they would enjoy great success in this land prepared especially for them. Deuteronomy is a powerful book filled with many great chapters. Chapters 6, 7, and 8 are my favorites.

Chapter 6 says:

These are the commands, decrees and laws the LORD your God directed me to teach you to observe in the land that you are crossing the Jordan to possess, so that you, your children and their children after them may fear the LORD your God as long as you live by keeping all his decrees and commands that I give you, and so that you may enjoy long life. Hear, Israel, and be careful to obey so that it may go well with you and that you may increase greatly in a land flowing with milk and honey, just as the LORD, the God of your ancestors, promised you.

Hear, O Israel: The LORD our God, the LORD is one. Love the LORD your God with all your heart and with all your soul and with all your strength. These commandments that I give you today are to be on your hearts. Impress them on your children. Talk about them when you sit at home and when you walk along the road, when you lie down and when you get up. Tie them as symbols on your hands and bind them on your foreheads. Write them on the doorframes of your houses and on your gates.

When the LORD your God brings you into the land he swore to your fathers, to Abraham, Isaac and Jacob, to give you—a land with large, flourishing cities you did not build, houses filled with all kinds of good things you did not provide, wells you did not dig, and vineyards and olive groves you did not plant—then when you eat and are satisfied, be careful that you do not forget the LORD, who brought you out of Egypt, out of the land of slavery.

Fear the LORD your God, serve him only and take your oaths in his name. Do not follow other gods, the gods of the peoples around you; for the LORD your God, who is among you, is a jealous God and his anger will burn against you, and he will destroy you from the face of the land. Do not put the LORD your God to the test as you did at Massah. Be sure to keep the commands of the LORD your God and the stipulations and decrees he has given you. Do what is right and good in the LORD's sight, so that it may go well with you and you may go in and take over the good land the LORD promised on oath to your ancestors, thrusting out all your enemies before you, as the LORD said.

In the future, when your son asks you, "What is the meaning of the stipulations, decrees and laws the LORD our God has commanded you?" tell him: "We were slaves of Pharaoh in Egypt, but the LORD brought us out of Egypt with a mighty hand. Before our eyes the LORD sent signs and wonders—great and terrible—on Egypt and Pharaoh and his whole household. But he brought us out from there to bring us in and give us the land he promised on oath to our ancestors. The LORD commanded us to obey all these decrees and to fear the LORD our God, so that we might always prosper and be kept alive, as is the case today. And if we are careful to obey all this law before the LORD our God, as he has commanded us that will be our righteousness."

Chapter 6 is loaded with incredible promises. Terms like, long life, may go well with you, increase greatly, cities you didn't build, houses filled with good things, and wells you didn't dig; don't come from the great "tightwad" in the sky. They are conceived in the heart of a loving Father who wants the best for His children just like you want for yours. They are incredible instructions given to fathers that are the keys for a successful and blessed family. Whenever you're with them. When you're taking them to ball practice or ballet practice, or just playing in the yard. When you're sitting down to eat or whether you're picking up fast food. When you put them to bed and when you wake them up. Whenever you're with them, impress upon their hearts: Me. Make worship of Me the norm. Tell them who I AM and tell them all I've done for you, and in the midst of this you'll find success. Build this into your family so strong that it will carry into the next generation. And Men of Standing, the same holds true today. He's still waiting on all who will break away from our comfort zone, our fear, our spiritual laziness and our Clark Kent mindset and take Him up on His word.

Men of Standing are forces of virtue and valor. Of strength and great courage. They're magnetic. They step into situations and make wrongs right. One of the most powerful things we can do is to invite God into our family's at the deepest and most intimate level. Don't just *incorporate* Him into your family like you would a television show or a family vacation. Stop acting like the average Christian, and have the guts to take Him completely at His word even if you have to stand alone. Invite Him in. Make Him number one. Seek the Kingdom of God first. Put Him at the very center of everything and watch what He will do.

Then we come to chapter 7 and the blessings and the commands intensify. You read how God wants to drive out the stronger nations that stand against them, and how they were never to make treaties with pagan people. They are told they are a people chosen by God out of all the other people on earth to be His people, His treasured possession. Because of His great love for them, He will bless them with health and wholeness. He'll bless the fruit of their womb, the crops of their land, and they will be blessed more than any other people. Then you come to Chapter 8, one of the most powerful verses in the Bible.

Be careful to follow every command I am giving you today, so that you may live and increase and may enter and possess the land the LORD promised on oath to your ancestors. Remember how the LORD your God led you all the way in the wilderness these forty years, to humble and test you in order to know what was in your heart, whether or not you would keep his commands. He humbled you, causing you to hunger and then feeding you with manna, which neither you nor your ancestors had known, to teach you that man does not live on bread alone but on every word that comes from the mouth of the LORD. Your clothes did not wear out and your feet did not swell during these forty years. Know then in your heart that as a man disciplines his son, so the LORD your God disciplines you.

Observe the commands of the LORD your God, walking in obedience to him and revering him. For the LORD your God is bringing you into a good land—a land with brooks, streams, and deep springs gushing out into the valleys and hills; a land with wheat and barley, vines and fig trees, pomegranates, olive oil and honey; a land where bread will not be scarce and you will lack nothing; a land where the rocks are iron and you can dig copper out of the hills.

When you have eaten and are satisfied, praise the LORD your God for the good land he has given you. Be careful that you do not forget the LORD your God, failing to observe his commands, his laws and his decrees that I am giving you this day. Otherwise, when you eat and are satisfied, when you build fine houses and settle down, and when your herds and flocks grow large and your silver and gold increase and all you have is multiplied, then your heart will become proud and you will forget the LORD your God, who brought you out of Egypt, out of the land of slavery. He led you through the vast and dreadful wilderness, that thirsty and waterless land, with its venomous snakes and scorpions. He brought you water out of hard rock. He gave you manna to eat in the wilderness, something your ancestors had never known, to humble and test you so that in the end it might go well with you. You may say to yourself, "My power and the strength of my hands have produced this wealth for me." But remember the LORD your God, for it is he who gives you the ability to produce wealth, and so confirms his covenant, which he swore to your ancestors, as it is today.

Read chapter 8 again. And then again. Discover the love of the Father, even after their disobedience. After all the grumbling and the complaining. After all the times they failed to trust, and they turned their back on God. He still created a promised land and a prosperous life for His children. What a picture of mercy. What a picture of love and grace.

Follow Me says the Father so you can live and increase. That you might enter and possess. God was teaching them that it wasn't just His plan for them to go live there but it was the indescribable desire of His heart for them to possess it also. To own it. To be much. To be many. To be blessed and to dominate in the land.

His love was so strong for them that even during the times of discipline He fed them every day with fresh manna, and for 40 years their clothes or their shoes never wore out. The Father takes care of His own. In his final moments, as Moses would read this book to the Israelites he began to describe in detail what they could expect in the Promise Land. A land that was filled with brooks and streams and deep gushing springs. Wheat, barley, figs, and olive oil. A land where precious metals could be dug from the ground, where bread would never be scarce and a land where they would lack nothing. Look closely at the last statement. A land where they would lack nothing. That's God's will.

And then you get to the latter part of the chapter where some of the most powerful words in all the word are written. Moses tells them to watch ever so closely when it all goes great for them. When harvest after harvest abounds for them. When they build and live in fine houses. When their number of livestock grow large and prosperous. When their bank account is bigger than it's ever been and their extremely rich. When everything they have is multiplied! Multiplied! God is a God of multiplication. When you are satisfied and life is going great, don't forget Me. Keep Me in the center of your lives. Because one day you may think all this came from the work of your hands alone, but never forget it was Me, the One who saw you. The One who never gave up on you. The One who led you through all your troubles who now gives you the power to produce wealth. That word "power" is the Hebrew word "Koach" and is better translated, strength, power, and might.

Then God tells them He gave them this strength, power and might in order that they might produce wealth, and so confirms His covenant. But here's the real meaning. Look at it closely in the Hebrew. God tells them it is He who gives them the power to produce "chayil". Standing! The same word used to describe Boaz in the book of Ruth is the exact same word the Creator of the universe uses to describe a life for all who will seek it. He says that He gives us the ability to produce "standing" so the covenant can be confirmed. God made a covenant with His children and gave them the ability to produce a life of means, resources, wealth, virtue, valor, strength, and ability. That's His covenant. That's His will and it's open today for all who will believe and receive. It's the Covenant of Standing!

This book is written for men but if "standing" were available to only to us then half of the world gets shortchanged from the destiny of life of standing. Boaz and Ruth, husband and wife, both man and women became people of standing. They made a home of standing and they lived out a destiny of standing. And so can we.

The Bible says in Ephesians 1:3 that if you are in Christ then you have been blessed with every spiritual blessing in the Heavenlies. Every spiritual blessing. And that included the blessing of "chayil," of Standing. It's yours. Take it. Receive it. Allow the awesome, indescribable God of the universe along with His perfect Son and His indwelling Spirit to explode this into your life so powerfully that the world comes to you to ask what has changed in your life. And not for your flesh to be honored but His name to be praised.

2 Peter 1:4 says God has given us His greatest and most precious and intimate promises in order that we may come onto the scene and live as a partner in the nature of God, and it's ours for the believing and receiving. Sadly, many of today's churches have fallen flat with the issue of the destiny that God has placed in all of us. And, Ephesians 2:10 in the Amplified Version says, "For we are God's [own] handiwork (His workmanship), recreated in Christ Jesus, [born anew] that we may do those good works which God predestined (planned beforehand)

There really is a "good life which He prearranged and made ready for us to live." There really is a "Zoe Perrisso" life He has made ready for us when we, once and for all, take Him at His word and receive and live it out to the full.

for us [taking paths which He prepared ahead of time], that we should walk in them [living the good life which He prearranged and made ready for us to live]."

There really is a "good life which He prearranged and made ready for us to live." There really is a "Zoe Perrisso" life He has made ready for us when we, once and for all, take Him at His word and receive and live it out to the full. There really is a Life of Standing for men and women that He has created and longs for all of His children to enter into and live out to the full.

Refuse to let the world rob you of this life. Reject any teachings that reject the words of Christ. Put on a limitless mindset and know that because of His indescribable love, God still stands ready for you to receive the destiny He has already created for you.

There's a river to cross. A river of doubts and fears; of useless, religious mindsets and worn our teaching. A river that will open up for us, just as the Jordan opened for all to cross over when the priest had stepped foot in it. Our Great High Priest has already stepped into that river, and we must have the strength and resolve to cross over on dry ground.

One last word and it's on a personal note. I started this chapter with the loss of a close friend and how he was a true Man of Standing, encouraging me to live out my mission, even to the end of his time here on earth. A few days after I emailed this manuscript to my literary agent so the publishing process could begin, I received a call from the kidney dialysis clinic where my father had been receiving his treatments for the past 6 months. My father had undergone some health issues with his heart and kidneys and now dialysis had become a part of his life. This was also a call I never wanted to receive. The nurse told me that his blood pressure was low, his heart rate was high and he was spitting up dried blood. They were calling an ambulance and taking him to the emergency room. I was literally right by the clinic on the highway so I quickly exited and headed to its location. My son Ryan was already there as well. They loaded him on the gurney and into the ambulance. As only God would plan it, my best friend who is an ER doctor was just arriving for his 6:00 pm to 6:00 am shift. I was texting him to keep him updated. They were going to allow me to ride with dad to the ER since it was literally across the street from the clinic. I stepped out the side door of the ambulance to tell my son to meet us at the hospital, but they quickly closed all the doors as something began to happen. Ryan looked inside and said that his granddad was panicking. In reality my dad was going into atrial fibrillation. Fifteen seconds later his heart got back into a normal rhythm and they let me back inside. Since I was a little boy my father had told me a saying, "Never get scared until you see me get scared." That saying helped me during many storms and a few west Texas tornadoes. This was the first time in my life I saw fear on my dad's face. With lights flashing and sirens screaming they headed just down the road where we were met by at the entrance by my doctor friend. Knowing he was there to take care of my dad gave me a sense of relief.

To know my dad was to know a man who had an incredible sense of humor and was the king of one-liners. As soon as they rolled him into the room his sense of humor kicked in and he began to joke with the hospital staff that was treating him. It appeared chaotic, as many people were running in and out of the room, at the same time they all knew their roles and were executing them with great precision. A few minutes later my dad said that he felt "so, so much better than he did a few minutes ago." A few seconds later one of the nurses asked him if he had any chest pain. This was probably the tenth time he had been asked that question, and each time his answer was no, but this time he said that he felt a little flutter in his chest. Thirty seconds later he was out.

The next forty minutes were painful. We looked on as they tried electrical shocks and violent CPR. By that time there were almost twenty family members and a couple of very close friends all waiting. A couple of reports had come back. His septic count and his hemoglobin count. Both were horrible. My friend came over to hug me as I cried, and told Liz and I that even if they could bring dad out of this trauma there was only a slim chance he'd ever leave the hospital. At 7:11 p.m. on April 7, 2015 my earthly hero went home to be with his bride of 51 years, and his two sons lost at birth, his parents, siblings, a multitude of family and friends, and his Savior. We gathered around him, held hands, prayed, and then sang him into glory.

Two days later I was sitting with one of my closest friends, who happened to be with us in the room. We were talking about all that had taken place. He was astounded by the number of people that were there in such a short amount of time. I told him I can't imagine what it would be like to die without any eternal hope, and to be a man who had left his family by his own mistakes and decisions, and was forced to die alone. To not have anyone to comfort him, no one to even hold his hand. My friend then became extremely surreal and began to picture the day he would find himself on that table. Would it just be him? Would his wife and kids be there or any of his friends? How many people will be standing by you when you die? It hit me like a ton of bricks and I said, "Could it be that the measure of a Man of Standing, is how many people are standing by when he goes into eternity?" How many has he touched in his lifetime that changed their lives and their destinies? How much leadership was shown? How much sacrifice? What kind of life will be portrayed

> *"Could it be that the measure of a Man of Standing, is how many people are standing by when he goes into eternity?"*

before his wife, children and the world? Now I believe stronger than ever that the measure of a man will be tallied in his last days and even his last minutes.

What about you? How many people will be there with you? How many will you have sacrificed for, both physically and financially? How many times will you arise in the middle of the night and spend hours in prayerful intercession for a person in need? How many will you mentor and lead, not only in word, but in example, so that they will say you were the one who made the difference in their lives?

There are thousands of books written by those who have mastered their mission and are now considered experts in their field. This is not one of those books. This is being written by a man who is on this journey to live out Standing and Zoe Perrisso. I'm no expert. I haven't mastered Standing but I've tasted just enough of what God called me to do to know this is my obsession. To know Him and the life He prearranged and made ready for me and my family to live. A life where He sent His only Son to be crucified and rise again so that we may truly know Him and live out His destiny for our lives. A life the most powerful Being in the universe longs for His children to enter into and celebrate with Him every day while making a mark in this world. But I have also discovered that this Superman life we all long to live will only be lived if we let the greatest Superman who ever walked the face of this earth to live His life through us and His name

Jesus the Christ. We can attempt to accomplish everything that's been written up to this point, but the only way it's truly possible to live it out and taste it all, is to allow the One who came to seek and save those who were lost live it through us. Let Him in. Let Him live His life through you. It's the only way Superman!

I said in the introduction I wrote this for you and your journey. I now realize that I have written this as a roadmap for me. I really hope you'll join me. I've watched as over an estimated three million men have risen up and spent time with their kids at school. But now I want to build a much larger network of men who will finally wake up to the truth of what God wants for them. To rise up to the occasion, to take off the clumsy clothes and the goofy glasses and let The Superman life, The Man of Standing Life change the destiny of not only himself, but of every member of his family. Join me, and let's go change the world. Rise up Man of Standing. All of creation groans for us to step up and step into our roll. It's the way it's supposed to be!

CPSIA information can be obtained at www.ICGtesting.com
Printed in the USA
LVOW07s1137240915

455505LV00001B/1/P